RUDOLF STEINER (1861–1925) called his spiritual philosophy 'anthroposophy', meaning 'wisdom of the human being'. As a highly developed seer, he based his work on direct knowledge and perception of spiritual dimensions. He initiated a modern and universal 'science of spirit', accessible to anyone willing to exercise clear and unprejudiced thinking.

From his spiritual investigations Steiner provided suggestions for the renewal of many activities, including education (both general and special), agriculture, medicine, economics, architecture, science, philosophy, religion and the arts. Today there are thousands of schools, clinics, farms and other organizations involved in practical work based on his principles. His many published works feature his research into the spiritual nature of the human being, the evolution of the world and humanity, and methods of personal development. Steiner wrote some 30 books and delivered over 6000 lectures across Europe. In 1924 he founded the General Anthroposophical Society, which today has branches throughout the world.

emanated from them. Everything which relates to the reproduction of humankind originated with them. In this they acted quite consciously, but the other human beings could only feel this influence as an instinct implanted in them. Sexual love was implanted in the human being by direct transference of thought. At first all its manifestations were of the noblest kind. Everything in this area which has taken on an ugly character comes from later times, when human beings became more independent and when they corrupted an originally pure instinct. In these older times there was no satisfaction of the sexual impulse for its own sake; everything at that time was a sacrificial service for the continuation of human existence. Reproduction was regarded as a sacred matter, as a service which human beings owed to the world. Sacrificial priests were the directors and regulators in this field.

The capacity of perpetuating the existence of his kind was implanted in the human being as an instinctive impulse by superhuman beings. Spiritually, the human being would have had to continue a sort of dream existence if the half-superhuman beings had not intervened. Through their influence, the images of his soul were directed towards the sensory external world. He became a being that was conscious of itself in the world of the senses. As a result it came about that the human being could consciously direct its actions in accordance with his perceptions of the world of the senses. Before this, he had acted from a kind of instinct. He had been under the spell of his external environment and of the powers of higher individualities which acted on him. Now he began to follow the impulses and enticements of his ideas. As a result, free choice became possible for the human being. This was the beginning of 'good and evil'.

SEXUALITY, LOVE AND PARTNERSHIP

From the Perspective of Spiritual Science

RUDOLF STEINER

Compiled and edited by Margaret Jonas

RUDOLF STEINER PRESS

Rudolf Steiner Press
Hillside House, The Square
Forest Row, RH18 5ES

www.rudolfsteinerpress.com

Published by Rudolf Steiner Press 2011

For earlier English publications, see Sources section on p. 241

Originally published in German in various volumes of the GA (*Rudolf Steiner Gesamtausgabe* or Collected Works) by Rudolf Steiner Verlag, Dornach. For further information see Sources, p. 241. This authorized translation is published by permission of the Rudolf Steiner Nachlassverwaltung, Dornach

All material has been translated or checked against the original German by Christian von Arnim

Translation and selection © Rudolf Steiner Press 2011

A catalogue record for this book is available from the British Library

ISBN: 978 1 85584 260 1

Cover by Andrew Morgan Design featuring a painting by Albrecht Dürer
Typeset by DP Photosetting, Neath, West Glamorgan
Printed and bound by Gutenberg Press Limited, Malta

MIX
Paper from
responsible sources
FSC® C022612

Contents

is indeed, notably in the middle period between death and a new birth. But now we grow increasingly aware of how this universe, with all its erstwhile majesty and greatness, is shrinking and contracting. The planets which we bear within us—planets in their weaving movement—become what then pulsates and surges through the human etheric body. The fixed stars of the zodiac become what forms our life of nerves and senses. All this is shrinking to become a body—spiritual to begin with, and then etheric. And not until it has grown quite tiny is it received into the mother's womb, there to be clothed with earthly matter.

Then comes the moment when we draw near to earthly life. We now feel the universe, which until recently was ours, vanishing from us. It shrinks and wanes, and this experience begets in us the longing to come down again to earth once more to unite with a physical body on the earth. [...] great universe we had before withdrawn [...] our striving [...] now therefore do we look to [...] a human being [...]

All this involves, however, quite another [...] between death and rebirth goes on for many centuries, and [...] a human being is born, say, in the twentieth century, his descent will have been prepared for gradually—even as early as the sixteenth century. All through this time he himself has, moreover, in a certain sense been working down into earthly conditions and events.

A distant great-grandfather of yours, way back in the sixteenth century, fell in love with a distant great-grandmother. They felt the urge to come together, and at this time you were already at work from spiritual worlds. And in the seventeenth century, when a less distant great-grandfather and great-grandmother loved each other, you once again were in a sense the mediator. In this way you accompanied [...] the

A deeply hidden interplay exists between the soul realm and the spirit sphere. Everywhere, soul longingly seeks spirit and is filled with bliss when it is allowed to draw close to it. This mysterious alternation of seeking and finding pervades all the kingdoms of nature and the human being. In nature, it is concealed in the miracle of the seasons: the earth seeks and finds heaven in spring and summer, and is separated from it again in autumn and winter. The seeking and finding of human beings who love one another is a revelation of the interplay between soul and spirit, holding sway in all creation. The love of the devout heart for God directly reveals this secret, but earthly love is only another aspect of the same phenomenon. In and above all earthly love, the longing, seeking and finding can become visible which guides the soul in the spirit and thereby, in a higher form, to itself.

Emil Bock, *The Song of Songs*, from *Kings and Prophets*[*]

---

[*]Translated by Maria St Goar, Floris Book, 1989.

much more likely to be led to that bond of brotherhood by something else, namely by spiritual knowledge itself. There is no other means of bringing about a universal human brotherhood than the spreading of esoteric knowledge through the world. One may talk for ever of Love and the Brotherhood of Mankind, one may found fraternities of fraternities, they will not lead to the desired goal, however well-intentioned they may be. The point is to use the right means, to know how to found this bond of brotherhood and sisterhood. Only those whose lives are grounded in universal, eternal, truth, valid for all human beings, find themselves together in the one truth. As the sun unites the plants which strive towards it while yet remaining individually separate, so does the truth to which all are striving. It is uniform; and then all human beings will come together. But they must strive energetically towards truth, for only then do they live together in harmony.

You might object that surely all are striving towards the truth, but that there are different standpoints, and that all strife and dissensions arise. This demonstrates insufficiently thorough knowledge of truth. One must understand that there may be different standpoints; one must first experience the truth itself and in itself; truth does not depend on whether a vote in its name is true in itself. Or would you put into the vote whether the three angles of a triangle do or do not add up to 180 degrees? Whether millions of people argue about this or not, it is settled; once when you have recognized it, it is made for you. There is no democracy about truth. Those who are not sufficiently mature, if one has not penetrated far enough into the truth, that is the origin of all dispute over truth. You might say, one may be of one opinion, this and another man of another esoteric viewpoint. In esoteric doctrine that is not so. It is the same wisdom

Introduction

It is with slight trepidation that we are offering this selection of extracts on the themes of sex and love, as it is far from any desire to appear salacious or sensational. When Rudolf Steiner was alive he could speak about love but was unable to say a great deal about sex, for apparently he could perceive the inner agitation of souls if he embarked on the topic. Presumably it would have been much more possible—and indeed asked of him—today. It was in any case not 'done' in the early twentieth century to speak freely on the subject beyond medical circles or in private. We live in very different times in which we cannot escape exposure to the stirring of the sexual in us at every opportunity and in almost every area of life. The sexual 'revolution' of the 1960s brought much that was good in relation to the status and needs of women and in opening up the pit to reveal the horrors of sexual abuse, which all along had been happening in secret. However they also ushered in the present increase in pornography, in the decline of taste and judgement regarding appropriate behaviour, language etc., and the darker prevalence of what had once seemed perverse and undignified human behaviour being presented—and encouraged—as the norm, something in fact Steiner warned would come about, whilst the other major decline has been in the stability of family life. But if readers are hoping for indications on contraception, abortion, homosexuality or transsexualism they will be disappointed. As far as I am aware no written records exist, and verbal references are of the flimsiest. Transsexualism or gender reassignment was not in any case possible medically then, though there were probably always some individuals who lived as the opposite gender.

Something of a sexual revolution had also begun by the latter part of Rudolf Steiner's life. People in artistic or 'bohemian' circles had long lived more freely, but the years following the First World War saw a breakdown of many of society's norms, women's emancipation grew and both sexes enjoyed a greater freedom to mix and choose their marriage partners. People complained of the decadence, especially in city life, as they still do, but few would want to return to the constraints of nineteenth-century society. Young people in Germany were throwing off these constraints and joining the *Wandervogel*[1] movement, rather like the hippies and students of the 1960s, seeking new freedoms in simplicity of dress, behaviour and outlook, and many were drawn to anthroposophy. Tragically their ideals were also exploited by the rise of Nazism. Steiner gave great encouragement to these young people, but was also aware of their vulnerability. This was daringly portrayed somewhat earlier by the German playwright Frank Wedekind's *Spring Awakening* (1891), which caused a scandal at the time for showing scenes of free adolescent sexuality, leading tragically to abortion and suicide. In Britain, in 1915 D.H. Lawrence's novel *The Rainbow* was suppressed on account of its 'indecency' and *Women in Love* was not published until 1921. There were other sexual theorists and experimental ways of living too. The notes to the conversations with the younger people drawn to anthroposophy in *Youth and the Etheric Heart*[2] give some interesting examples. These conversations, however, barely touch on the theme and the replies are more fully dealt with in the extracts here.

These extracts attempt to show how at the time in evolution known as the 'Fall'[3] the interference of adversary beings Steiner calls luciferic caused a change to come about in the human being, who hitherto had been a single sexed entity and who then gradually became split into two with the beginning of reproduction as we know it. This stage is echoed in embryology when the fertilized egg only displays secondary sex characteristics from an undifferentiated form, but otherwise it is familiar to us in myths such as described in Plato's *Symposium*.[4] After this, we are to learn through suffering our sexual nature, according to Rudolf Steiner, in order to achieve higher stages of human love. He even indicates that reproduction will happen differently in the distant future and a more androgynous human being will emerge as the female grows more barren. There are hints of this future androgyny today in the more boyish form of many women and the reduced fertility in both sexes.

In various lectures on cultural evolution Rudolf Steiner speaks about an earlier stage of history when women had greater dominance or valued positions in society and how this had altered by the period he called the fourth post-Atlantean epoch (747 BC–AD 1413),[5] partly overlapping with the Iron Age. Male dominance then became the norm, especially reflected in Graeco-Roman times, and remained largely unchallenged until about the eighteenth century. By the beginning of the twentieth century, however, a woman's movement had begun in earnest—'the woman question' as it was put. We have to remember how rare it was then for a woman to have a profession and that suffrage was not granted to all women until 1928 in Great Britain and 1920 in the USA, although New Zealand granted it in 1893 and Finland was the first European country to do so in 1906. Rudolf Steiner was certainly in the vanguard of his time in 1894 when he stated that it was up to women themselves to determine what they could achieve. He had the highest regard for his female co-workers, amongst whom were the speech artist Marie Steiner-von Sivers, the medical doctor Ita Wegman and the astronomer Elisabeth Vreede. When asked to found the movement for religious renewal known as the Christian Community, he made it clear from the outset that there were to be women priests ordained with equal status to the men—the first Christian Church to make this possible, something still unacceptable to many branches of Christianity (and indeed some other faiths). He pointed to a time, already coming about, when women would again assume significant positions in society.

With respect to children's sexuality, Steiner was adamant that the young child is not a sexual being—this only develops towards adolescence. We should remember that Freud's ideas were already prevailing at this time with the notion of an infant sexuality, the Oedipus complex and childish sexual fantasies of abuse (which in hindsight may not necessarily have been fantasies at all). Thus the 'innocence' of childhood beloved by the Victorians was disappearing fast. If today one might question Steiner's remarks here, it could be as a result of culture and fashion that young children appear sexualized, and of a society which harshly criminalizes anyone whose weaknesses lead them to fall into temptation. Whilst not in any way condoning their behaviour, it would surely be a wise move if society were to look at what it is doing to children and how this trend is also a form of abuse.

It is about the confusion of sex and love that we can really learn to think differently. In our time, sadly, 'love' usually means 'sex', so that same-sex friendships are constantly viewed with salaciousness or suspicion, and even to comfort a distressed child other than one's own with an embrace is to risk prosecution. The current assumption that one cannot 'love' without physically desiring another person greatly needs to be challenged.

Certain beings are at work in our sexuality and of these Rudolf Steiner again said little beyond some of the influences of the main adversary beings he referred to as Lucifer and Ahriman. Lucifer, whose aim is to lead souls away from the earth to his own realm, inspires the yearning of romantic love. Ahriman, whose aim is to bind souls more firmly to the earth, encourages the physical side of desire—sex without love. Because of the way in which sexuality is linked with our metabolism, in which beings of a destructive nature play an important part in the breaking down of food substance, we can assume the presence of other elemental beings which have a role that is partly destructive but also creative—as in the case of reproduction. It is when they spill over into areas beyond their 'remit' that they become evil. In lectures given in England in 1924,[6] Steiner indicated some of the aberrations connected with these elementals, especially in relation to human fluid emanations. With regard to the practice of sex in spiritual life, his view was that this is not the modern path of development. It may have been possible without polluting the soul in ancient cultures such as the original Indian, but an increased 'fall' of the beings involved in such practices has come about, with a different connection to the blood and nerves. Subjects such as 'tantric' sex he did not speak about, and the assertion sometimes made that he belonged to the Ordo Templi Orientis (OTO), which practised this, is a misunderstanding of the tenuous connection between his early ritual Lodge and this order, which only somewhat later was taken over by figures such as Aleister Crowley and used for magical tantric practices.[7]

In the anthroposophical spiritual path of development, the chakras or 'lotus flowers' are unfolded from above downwards and Steiner warned against the danger of a prematurely awakened kundalini. As the extracts from *Community Life, Inner Development, Sexuality and the Spiritual Teacher* make clear, sexuality should be kept apart from the spiritual life. However this does not make him an ascetic. He was not preaching chastity, nor following St Paul by saying 'It is better to marry than burn'. It is much more a matter of coming to understand what we are doing, as his reply to Elsa Kriewitz shows. She had asked him in 1921 if an anthroposophist should renounce sensual love. He replied: 'Ganz anders ist es! Alles dürfen Sie! Lieben, heiraten, sich scheiden lassen—*nur wissen müssen Sie, was Sie tun! Das ist notwending!*'[8] (On the contrary! You can do everything! Love, marry, divorce—*you just have to be aware of what you are doing! That is essential!*)

As these passages hopefully reveal, sex is a necessary stage of human evolution. How we handle it determines our stage of inner development—though, as in the case of Goethe, Steiner was perfectly able to acknowledge Goethe's genius whilst recognizing the 'all-too-human' which prevailed in his personal life. This split in the human being he described as a fact of our age. The healing of it will only happen gradually. The story of Parzival bringing healing to Amfortas by finally asking the Grail question of what ailed him—his wounded groin being a metaphor for sexual misadventures—this story, though medieval in origin, is in fact the one for our time, showing how we can proceed. In a lecture of 7 February 1913, given in Berlin (not included here),[9] Rudolf Steiner makes the connection between Goethe's dual nature and the wounded Amfortas as reflecting the plight of the modern human being. Parzival, the bearer of the 'consciousness soul' forces is the one who can heal him. Amfortas is healed by love and compassion and the renewing life forces of the Grail. The main protagonists achieve wholeness through marriage: Parzival has remained true to Condwiramur, Gawain overcomes his lower passions, and Feirefiz comes to the Grail by loving the Grail-bearer. The valuable insights of C.G. Jung have shown us how our soul life needs to unite the male and female qualities within us to achieve wholeness, an inner marriage again hinted at much earlier by Johann Valentin Andreae's *Chymical Wedding of Christian Rosenkreutz* (1616).[10] Rudolf Steiner presents the human soul dilemma, split into male and female attributes, and also with regard to both sexes split within itself, but offers a path of development which will eventually lead to overcoming these—what Jung called 'individuation', a merging with the true self or true ego of the human being.

*

In making this selection I must gratefully acknowledge the spadework provided by Richard Lewis in a privately printed compilation *Love, Marriage, Sex in the Light of Spiritual Science* (undated). His thoroughness in his search for extracts has proved invaluable. The translations used here are not his, however, but in most cases are revised from the original English editions.

The selection does not claim to be exhaustive. For instance, the interesting but rather specialized material from the lecture series *The Temple Legend*[11] has not been included as it is lengthy and its context within Freemasonry would take us further from the theme.

Margaret Jonas

1. The Division into Two Sexes and Reproduction

In these six extracts Rudolf Steiner describes the earlier stages of the earth's evolution, in particular the period known as Lemuria[12] when the division into two sexes began to occur, at a time when the moon separated from the earth. Reproduction started to take place differently, at first more unconsciously, directed by spiritual beings, until the Atlantean epoch when human beings began to be aware of a more sensual attraction to one another. Steiner stresses that although humanity had 'fallen' due to the influence of luciferic beings, reproduction should not be seen as pernicious; it is the misuse of these forces which can lead to evil. This is in contrast to the medieval Church's view that human sexuality was intrinsically evil— though a necessary one.

The last two extracts discuss the process of incarnation: how souls seek to incarnate, how they can perceive the love feelings of prospective parents and—even more importantly—are active together with spiritual beings in bringing about a couple's relationship. The idea that souls choose their parents and influence them is an important part of understanding how we pass through successive earth lives. Steiner was anxious that the term 'unbornness' should enter our languages.[13] Here he gives meaning to it. Moreover by working with the beings of the zodiac and planets we prepare our descent from the spiritual world often for centuries in advance and influence the marital choices of our ancestors to a remarkable degree. The final extract describes the future of human reproduction. Steiner was aware that it sounds extraordinary—we can only live with the idea.

1.1 The division of the sexes

The moment in human evolution we want to recall lies a long way back. If we go back through post-Atlantean times and then through Atlantean times as far as ancient Lemuria, we come to that moment when the division of the sexes took place in the human realm on earth. You know that before this we cannot speak of such a division of the sexes in the human realm. I want to emphasize that we are not speaking of the very first appearance altogether of two sexes in earthly evolution or in evolution as a whole, in so far as it comprises the realms that are around us. Phenomena that certainly involve two genders occur earlier. But what we call the human realm did not divide into two genders until Lemurian times. Prior to that the human shape was formed differently, and both sexes were in a way contained within it in an undifferentiated way. We can form an external picture of the transition from dual sexuality to the division into sexes if we visualize how the earlier dual gendered human being gradually developed in such a way that in one group of individuals the characteristics of the one sex, the female, became more pronounced, whilst in the other group the characteristics of the male sex developed more strongly. This was still a long time before the sexes separated, when there was progressive development in one direction or the other, at a time when man still lived in a very insubstantial material body.

We have focused our attention on this moment in time to start with because we want to enquire into the meaning of why the two sexes arose. It is only when we have a spiritual-scientific basis that we can enquire into such meaning, for physical evolution receives its meaning from higher worlds.

As long as we are in the physical world, it is somewhat childish to talk of purpose if we consider it from a philosophical perspective. And Goethe and others were right to make fun of the people who talked of the purpose in nature, as though nature in her wisdom had created cork so that human beings could make stoppers with it. This is a childish way of looking at things and can only lead to our missing the main point at issue. This view would be similar to thinking of a clock as having little demonic beings behind it wise enough to make the hands go round. In actual fact if we want to know how the clock works we must go to the mind that produced it, namely the clockmaker. And similarly when we want to understand purpose in our world we must step beyond the physical world and enter the spiritual. Thus purpose, meaning and goal are words that we can apply to evolution only when we consider them on a spiritual-scientific basis. It is in this sense that we ask the question: what is the meaning behind the two sexes gradually developing and then interacting?

The meaning will become clear to you when you see what we call fertility, the reciprocal influence of the sexes, replacing something else that had previously existed. You must not think that fertility appeared for the first time at the moment when the division into sexes occurred in human evolution. That was not so. We must picture to ourselves that in the times preceding dual sexuality this fertility took place in quite a different way. Clairvoyant vision can see that there was a time in humankind's earthly evolution when fertility happened in connection with the intake of food, and those beings which in those early times were male-female received fertilizing forces with their food. This food was still of course of a much more delicate nature, and when human beings partook of nourishment in those times there was something else contained in these nourishing fluids which gave these beings the possibility of producing another being of like kind. You must realize, however, that the nourishing fluids taken from the substance of their surroundings did not always contain these fertilizing fluids, but only at quite definite times. This depended on the changes that took place which are comparable to today's seasonal changes, changes of climate, and so on. The nourishing foods imbibed from the surroundings by these beings of a dual sexual nature had the power of fertilization at quite definite times.

If with clairvoyant consciousness we look further back still, we find another peculiarity in the propagation of ancient times. What you know today as the difference between the various individualities, which expresses itself in the multi-formity of life in our present cycle of humanity, these differences did not exist before the sexes came about. A great uniformity was there then. The beings that arose then were similar to one another and to their forefathers. All these beings that were still undivided into two sexes were outwardly very similar, and their characters were more or less the same too. That human beings were so much alike did not have the disadvantage in those times that it would have in the present time. Just imagine how infinitely dull human life would be if people were to come into the world today with identical appearance and character, and how little could actually happen in human life, as everybody would want to do the same thing as everybody else. But in ancient times this was not the case. When the human being was still as it were more etheric, more spiritual, and not so firmly embedded in matter, then at birth and on into childhood human beings were really very similar to one another, and the teachers would not have needed to notice whether the one child was a scamp and the other a gentle little being. Although the people were different in character at different times, they were in a certain way all fundamentally alike. Each person, however, did not remain the same throughout his life. Because the human being was still in a softer, more spiritual body, he was much more open to the permanent influences coming from the environment, so that in those ancient times these influences brought about tremendous changes in him. The human being became individualized in a certain way because, having a nature as soft as wax, he became more or less an impress of his surroundings. At a quite definite time in his life, which would coincide nowadays with puberty, it became possible for him to let everything that happened in his environment work upon him. The difference between the various periods that were comparable to our present-day seasons was very great, and it was of great importance to a man whether he lived in one part of the earth or another. If he travelled just a short distance over the earth, that had a great influence on him. If people go on a long journey nowadays they return on the whole the same as when they went away, however much they see (unless they are very impressionable). This was different in olden times. Everything had the greatest influence on people, and as long as they had a body of soft material they could actually become gradually individualized in the course of their life. Then this possibility ceased.

Something further that reveals itself to us is that the earth itself became denser and denser, and to the same extent as the substance—let us say the earthy nature of the earth— intensified this uniformity became harmful. For it gradually reduced the human being's capacity to change. He became very dense at birth, as it were. This is the reason why people nowadays change so little during their life. And this led Schopenhauer[14] to think that people were absolutely incapable of bringing about any basic changes in their character. The reason for this is that human beings are embodied in such dense substance. They cannot easily work on the substance or change it. If, as once was the case, human beings could still alter their limbs at will, make them long or short according to their need, then the human being would, of course, still be very impressionable. Then he would really be able to incorporate into his individuality the power to change himself. The human being is always in inner contact with his environment, especially his human environment. To clarify this, I would like to tell you something that you may not have noticed before but which is nevertheless true.

Imagine you are sitting facing someone and speaking to him. We are referring to ordinary human relationships in the normal course of life and not to someone who has a special and profound esoteric training. Two people are sitting together, one talking and the other just listening. It is generally imagined that the one who is listening is not doing anything. But that is not true. In things like this we still see the influence of the environment. It is not noticeable to outer perception, but inwardly it is very clear, in fact striking, that the one who is merely listening is joining in everything the other one is doing.

He even imitates the movements of the vocal cords and speaks with the speaker. Everything you hear you also say with a gentle movement of the vocal cords and the other speech organs. It makes a great difference whether the speaker has a croaky voice and those are the movements you have to imitate or whether he has a pleasant voice. In this respect the human being does everything the other person is doing, and as this is really happening all the time it has a great influence on a person's whole development, though only in this limited respect. If you imagine this last residue of the human being's participation in his surroundings increased to a vast extent, you get an idea of how a person in ancient times lived and felt with his environment. The human being's faculty of imitation, for instance, was developed on a tremendous scale. If one person made a gesture, then everyone else made the same gesture too. Only a few insignificant things in certain particular directions remain of this today, like for instance when one person yawns other people do too. But remember that in these ancient times it was entirely a question of their having a dim consciousness with which this power of imitation was connected.

Now as the earth and everything upon it became denser and denser, the human being became less and less capable of transforming himself through the influence of his environment. In comparatively late Atlantean times a sunrise, for instance, had a powerfully creative effect upon the human being, because he was completely open to its influence and underwent sublime inner experiences, which if they continually recurred changed him tremendously in the course of his life. This diminished more and more and gradually disappeared altogether the more humanity progressed.

In Lemurian times, before the moon left the earth, humankind was in a dangerous predicament. It was in danger of becoming rigid to the point of mummification. Through the gradual departure of the moon from the evolution of the earth this danger was averted. At the same time as the moon departed, however, the division into sexes took place, and with this division came a new impulse for the individualization of the human being. If it had been possible for human

beings to propagate without the two sexes, this individualizing would not have taken place. The present diversity
among human beings is due to the interaction of the sexes. If
there were only the female element, human individuality
would be extinguished and human beings would all become
alike. Through the cooperation of the male element, human
beings are individual characters from birth. So the significance and meaning of the interaction of the sexes is to be
found in the fact that through the separation of the male
element the individualizing of the human being at birth has
replaced the old kind of individualization. What was achieved
in earlier times by the whole surrounding environment was
compressed into the interaction of the sexes, so that individualization was pushed back to the creation of the physical
human being at birth. That is the significance of the interaction of the two sexes. Individualization happens by way of
the effect of the male gender on the female.

Spirits overshadowed the human being and stimulated
him to bring forth his kind, and this was also experienced and
seen as a spiritual process.

Then, little by little, it became impossible for human
beings to see the spiritual in their environment. It became
more and more veiled from sight, especially during their day
consciousness. Little by little human beings lost sight of the
spirit behind things and they only perceived the external
objects which are the outer expression of these. They learnt
to forget the spiritual background and the influence of the
spirit grew less and less the denser the human being's body
became. Through this densification the human being
became a more and more independent being and shut himself off from his spiritual surroundings. The further we go
back into these ancient times the more spiritually godlike was

this influence that came from the surroundings. Human beings were really organized in such a way that they were a likeness of the spiritual beings present round them in their environment—images of the gods who in older times were present on earth.

Through the interaction of the two sexes, in particular, this was increasingly lost and the spiritual world withdrew from human beings' sight. Human beings beheld the sense world more and more clearly. We must picture this situation vividly. Just imagine, in those times the human being was fertilized from the spiritual world of the gods. It was the gods themselves who gave forth their forces and made people like themselves. That is why in those ancient times what we call illness did not exist. There was no inner disposition to illness and it could not be there because everything that was in the human being and that worked on him came from the health-giving divine-spiritual cosmos. The divine-spiritual beings are full of health and in those days they made human beings in their image. The human being was healthy. But the nearer he came to the time when the interaction of the sexes came about, and together with it the withdrawal of the spiritual worlds, and the more independent and individual the human being became, the more the health of divine-spiritual beings withdrew from him and something else took its place. What happened in reality was that such interaction of the sexes was accompanied by passions and instincts aroused in the physical world. We must look for this stimulus in the physical world after human beings had reached the point when the two sexes were sensually attracted to one another. This was a long time after the sexes already existed. The effect of the sexes one upon the other—even in Atlantean times—happened when physical consciousness was actually asleep during the night. It was not until the middle of the Atlantean period that what we call the attraction of the sexes began, what we might call passionate love—that is, sensual love that mingled with pure supersensual or platonic love. There would be much more platonic love if sensual love did not enter into it. And whereas everything that formerly helped to form the human being came from the divine-spiritual environment, it now came more from the passions and instincts of the two sexes working one upon the other. The kind of sensual longing that is stimulated by seeing the outer appearance of the opposite sex is bound up with the working together of the two sexes. And therefore something was incorporated into the human being at birth that is connected with the particular kind of passions and feelings human beings have in physical life. Whilst in earlier times the human being still received what was in him from the divine-spiritual beings of his surroundings, he now acquired something through the act of fertilization which, as an independent, self-contained being, he had taken into himself from the world of the senses.

After human beings had separated into two sexes, they passed on to their descendants what they themselves experienced in the sense world. So we now have two types of human being. These two types live in the physical world and perceive the world through their senses, and this leads them to develop various externally triggered impulses and long-ings, especially those arising from their own externally stimulated sensual attraction to one another. What now confronts a person in an external way has been drawn down into the sphere of the independent human being, and it is no longer in full harmony with the divine-spiritual cosmos. It is imparted to human beings through the act of fertilization; it is implanted in them. And this worldly life of theirs, received not from the world of the gods but from the external side of the divine-spiritual world, is passed on to their offspring through fertilization. If a person is bad in this respect, then he passes worse qualities on to his descendants than another person who is good and pure.

1.2 The transformation of the human form and the forces of reproduction

This change goes hand in hand with a transformation of the human form. One half of this form, together with two organs of movement, now becomes the lower half of the body, which functions mainly as the carrier of nutrition and reproduction. The other half of this form is turned upward, so to speak. The remaining two organs of movement become the rudiments of hands. Those organs which previously had served for nutrition and reproduction are transformed into organs of speech and thought. The human being has become upright. This is the immediate consequence of the separation of the moon. With the moon all those forces disappeared from the earth through which, during the fire-mist period, the human being could still fertilize himself and produce beings like himself without external influence. His whole lower half—that which we often call the lower nature—now came under the rational formative influence of higher beings. What these beings could previously regulate within the human being when the mass of forces now split off with the moon was still combined with the earth they now had to organize through the inter-action of the two sexes. It is therefore understandable that the moon is regarded by initiates as the symbol of the repro-ductive force. After all, these forces adhere to it, so to speak.

The higher beings we have described have an affinity with the moon, are in a sense moon gods. Before the separation of the moon they acted within the human being through its power; afterwards their forces acted from outside on human reproduction. One could also say that those noble spiritual forces which previously had acted on the still higher impulses of the human being through the medium of the fire-mist had now descended in order to exercise their power in the area of reproduction. Noble and divine forces do indeed exercise a regulating and organizing activity in this area.

This reflects an important proposition of esoteric teaching, namely that the higher, more noble divine forces have an affinity with the—apparently—lower forces of human nature. The word 'apparently' must here be understood in its full significance. For it would be a complete misconception of esoteric truths if one were to see something base in the forces of reproduction as such. Only when the human being misuses these forces, when he compels them to serve his passions and instincts, is there something destructive in them, but not when he ennobles them through the insight that a divine-spiritual power lies in them. Then he will place these forces at the service of the development of the earth, and through his forces of reproduction he will carry out the intentions of the higher beings we have characterized. Esoteric science teaches that this whole area should be ennobled, should be placed under divine laws, but not be made to die off. The latter can only be the consequence of esoteric principles that have been understood in a purely external fashion and distorted into a misconceived asceticism.

The heart, which after all is also a muscle, constitutes an exception to this general condition. In the present period of human development, the heart is not subject to voluntary movement, yet it is a 'striated' muscle. The science of the spirit indicates the reason for this. The heart will not always remain as it is now. In the future it will have a quite different form and a changed function. It is on the way to becoming a voluntary muscle. In the future it will execute movements that will be the effects of the inner soul impulses of the human being. The present structure already shows what significance it will have in the future, when the movements of the heart will be as much an expression of the human will as the lifting of the hand or the advancing of the foot are today.

This conception of the heart is connected with a comprehensive insight of the science of the spirit into the relation of the heart to the so-called circulation of the blood. The mechanical-materialistic view of life sees in the heart a kind of pumping mechanism which drives the blood through the body in a regular manner. Here the heart is the cause of the movement of the blood. The insight of the science of the spirit shows something quite different. From such a perspective, the pulsing of the blood and its whole inner mobility are the expression and the effect of the processes of the soul. The soul is the cause of the behaviour of the blood. Turning pale through feelings of fear, blushing under the influence of sensations of shame are coarse effects of soul processes in the blood. Everything that takes place in the blood is only the expression of what takes place in the life of the soul. However, the connection between the pulsation of the blood and the impulses of the soul is a deeply mysterious one. The movements of the heart are not the cause but the consequence of the pulsation of the blood. In the future, the heart will carry what takes place in the human soul into the external world through voluntary movements.

Other organs which are in a similarly ascending development are those of respiration in their function as instruments of speech. At present the human being can use them to transform his thoughts into air waves. He thereby impresses upon the external world what he experiences within himself. He transforms his inner experiences into air waves. This wave motion of the air is a rendering of what takes place within him. In the future, he will in this way give external form to more and more of his inner being. The final result in this direction will be that through his speech organs, which have arrived at the height of their perfection, he will produce his own kind. Thus the speech organs at present contain within themselves the future organs of reproduction in an embryonic state. The fact that a transformation (change of voice) occurs in the male individual at the time of puberty is a consequence of the mysterious connection between the instruments of speech and reproduction.

One could, for instance, proceed to draw the following conclusion from the description given above: because the human organs of reproduction in their present form will in the future be the first to lose their importance, they therefore were the first to acquire it in the past. Hence they are in a sense the oldest organs of the human body. Just the contrary of this is true. They were the last to receive their present form and will be the first to lose it again.

The following presents itself to spiritual-scientific research. On the Sun,[15] the physical human body had in a certain respect moved up to the level of plant existence. At that time it was permeated only by an etheric body. On the Moon[16] it took on the character of the animal body because it was permeated by the astral body. But not all organs participated in this transformation into animal character. A number of parts remained on the plant level. On the Earth, after the integration of the 'I', when the human body elevated itself to its present form, a number of parts were still decidedly plantlike in character. But one must not imagine that these organs looked exactly like our present-day plants. The organs of reproduction belong to these organs. They still exhibited a plantlike character at the beginning of Earth development. This was known to the wisdom of the ancient mysteries. Older art, which has retained so much of the traditions of the mysteries, represents hermaphrodites with plant-leaf-like organs of reproduction. These are precursors of the human being which still had the old kind of reproductive organs (which were double-sexed). This can be seen clearly, for example, in a hermaphrodite figure in the Capitoline Collection in Rome. When we look into such matters, we will also understand, for instance, the true reason for the presence of the fig-leaf on Eve. We will comprehend true explanations for many old representations, while contemporary interpretations are, after all, only the result of a thinking which is not carried to its conclusion. We shall only remark in passing that the hermaphrodite figure mentioned above shows still other plant appendages. When it was created, the tradition had still been passed down that in a very remote past certain human organs changed from plant to animal character.

1.3 The influence of higher beings and the sexual impulse

When the time came in which the sexes separated, spiritual beings considered it their task to act upon the new life in accordance with their mission. The regulation of sexual life emanated from them. Everything which relates to the reproduction of humankind originated with them. In this they acted quite consciously, but the other human beings could only feel this influence as an instinct implanted in them. Sexual love was implanted in the human being by direct transference of thought. At first all its manifestations were of the noblest kind. Everything in this area which has taken on an ugly character comes from later times, when human beings became more independent and when they corrupted an originally pure instinct. In these older times there was no satisfaction of the sexual impulse for its own sake. Everything at that time was a sacrificial service for the continuation of human existence. Reproduction was regarded as a sacred matter, as a service which human beings owed to the world. Sacrificial priests were the directors and regulators in this field.

The capacity of perpetuating the existence of his kind was implanted in the human being as an instinctive impulse by superhuman beings. Spiritually, he would at first have had to continue a sort of dream existence if the half-superhuman beings had not intervened. Through their influence the images of his soul were directed towards the sensory external world. He became a being that was conscious of itself in the world of the senses. As a result it came about that the human being could consciously direct his actions in accordance with his perceptions of the world of the senses. Before this he had acted from a kind of instinct. He had been under the spell of his external environment and of the powers of higher individualities, which acted on him. Now he began to follow the impulses and enticements of his ideas. As a result, free choice became possible for the human being. This was the beginning of 'good and evil'.

1.4 Conception and the human being before birth

Everywhere in the astral world a clairvoyant sees souls who want to incarnate. Conditions of space and time in the astral world are of course different from those in the physical world. Such a soul can move with tremendous rapidity in the astral world and is impelled by certain forces to the locality where a physical and an etheric body befitting this soul are produced. Distance such as that between Budapest and New York plays no part whatever. Time factors come into consideration only in so far as the earthly possibilities of the most favourable conditions for incarnation can be achieved. From the earth there comes to this soul (which looks bell-shaped, widening from above downwards, as it flies through astral space) the physical element produced by the line of heredity.

We must now speak briefly of what draws the soul down to the earth and what it is that will incarnate. You know that procreation is connected with certain impulses of feeling, impulses of love, sympathy born of love. The process of procreation is preceded by sympathy born of love, which is perceived by a clairvoyant as a play of astral forces, of astral streams, between the man and the woman, surging back and forth. Something is alive there that is not present if the human being is alone; the companionship between the souls themselves is expressed in the play of the astral streams. But of course every process of love is individual and issues from a specific individuality. Now, before earthly fertilization, before the physical act of love, there is reflected in this play of astral forces the individuality, the being who is coming down again to the earth. That is the essential reality in the pro-creative act. So one can say that before physical fertilization what is descending from the spiritual world is already beginning to be active. The spiritual world is also instrumental in bringing about the meeting of the man and woman. A wonderfully intimate play of forces from the spiritual world is involved here. The being who is descending is, generally speaking, connected from the beginning with the product of fertilization. It is emphatically not the case that an individuality connects with it only after a certain time. From the moment of conception this individuality is in touch with the outcome of physical procreation. There are exceptions, of course, here too. During the first days after conception, this spiritual individuality who is descending does not yet actually affect the development of the physical human being, but it is close by, as it were, is already in contact with the developing embryo. The actual attachment takes place from about the eighteenth, nineteenth, twentieth and twenty-first days after conception; what is descending from a higher world is then already working together with the being who is in process of coming into existence. Thus the delicate, organic texture that is necessary if the human individuality is to use the physical body as an instrument is prepared from the beginning in accordance with the previous faculties. That the human being is an integrated unity originates from the fact that the smallest organ is in keeping with the organism as a whole, that is to say, even the smallest unit must be such that the whole structure is able to ensure that from the eighteenth to the twenty-first day after conception, the ego can participate in the development of the physical and etheric bodies.

Now to what extent does what is physically procreated, what the parents contribute, the female and male element, influence the development of the human being coming into existence? If you study in esoteric and spiritual terms what underlies the physical product, a great deal will become clear to you; naturally only the essentials can be touched upon here. We shall hear presently that in earlier times, before the separation of the sexes, procreation took place without participation by the male. If it were still the same today, what would happen? If the female element alone were to participate in the process of human procreation, what would occur? What is the involvement of the female element as such? If the female element alone were to operate, evolution would result in the child resembling its forebears to the greatest possible extent. Beings coming into existence would all be completely homogeneous. The principle of generality, homogeneity, originates from the female element. Only through the separation of the sexes has it become possible for human individuality to develop, for it is due to the influence of the male that the descendant is distinct from his forebears. The male element provides individuality.

As a result, successive incarnations or reincarnations were not possible until dual sexuality had been established on the earth. Not until then was the human being able to incarnate on the earth the product of earlier existence. That there is harmony between what occurs below on the earth and the individual entity who must evolve and be enriched from incarnation to incarnation is due to the fact that the male element and the female element work together. The human ego would no longer find a suitable body today if the universal human principle were not modified by the activity of the male element, that is to say, if the universal type were not individualized. It is essentially the etheric body that is worked upon by the female element. In the etheric body, where the permanent tendencies are rooted, the driving force of the female element is at work. The principle of generality, of the generic, is anchored in the etheric body. In the etheric body

of the woman there is still present today the counterpart of
what exists outwardly as the folk soul, the spirit of the ethnic
group. Folk soul and spirit of the ethnic group are similar to
one another.

If we now bear in mind the spiritual reality underlying
conception, we must say that conception in itself is nothing
other than a kind of deadening of the living forces of the
etheric body. Death, at conception, is already woven into the
human body. It is an event that hardens, as it were, and
deadens the etheric body, which otherwise would multiply ad
infinitum.

The etheric body, which originates from the female principle and would otherwise produce copies only, is densified
as a result of the male influence and thereby becomes the
creator of the new human individuality. Procreation consists
in the production of a copy of the etheric body of the woman;
through being hardened, in a certain respect killed, it is at the
same time individualized. In the deadened etheric body there
lies hidden the formative force that produces the new human
being. In this way conception and procreation amalgamate.
Thus we see that two conceptions take place: below, physical,
human conception; above, the conception of the archetype as
the result of its own karma. We said that from the eighteenth
to the twenty-first day after conception the ego is already
working on the embryo; but not until much later, after six
months, do other forces also work on the embryo, forces that
determine the karma of the human being. This can be
expressed by saying that the web woven out of karma takes
hold at that point; gradually these forces come into play. Now
exceptions occur here, too, so that later on an exchange of
the ego may take place. We will speak of that later. The ego is
the first factor to intervene for the purpose of development.

If we want to have an approximate picture of what exists in the spiritual world and is about to descend, we must say that it is the individual who is in the process of incarnating who brings together those who love one another. The archetype wishing to incarnate has drawn to itself the astral substance and that now affects the passionate feeling of love. The astral passion surging back and forth on the earth below mirrors the astral substances of the descending entity. So the astral substance coming from above is met by the astral feeling of those who love each other, which is itself influenced by the substance of the entity descending to incarnation. When we think this thought to its conclusion, we must say that the reincarnating individual definitely participates in the choice of his parents. According to who and what he is, he is drawn to the parental couple concerned. One might well object that if the choosing of parents were accepted as a fact the feeling of finding a new life in one's children would be lost and that the love based upon having transmitted something of one's own to them would thereby be lessened. This is a groundless fear, for maternal and paternal love assume a higher and more beautiful meaning when we realize that in a certain sense the child loves the parents even before conception and is thereby drawn to them. The parents' love is therefore the answer to the child's love, it is the responsive love. We have thus an explanation of parental love as the reproduction of the child's love that precedes the physical birth.

1.5 Incarnation and its influence on human relationships

The nearer we approach a new earthly life, the more does this universe which is the human being contract for us. Majestic it is indeed, notably in the middle period between death and a new birth. But now we grow increasingly aware of how this universe, with all its erstwhile majesty and greatness, is shrinking and contracting. The planets which we bear within us—planets in their weaving movement—become what then pulsates and surges through the human etheric body. The fixed stars of the zodiac become what forms our life of nerves and senses. All this is shrinking to become a body—spiritual to begin with, and then etheric. And not until it has grown quite tiny is it received into the mother's womb, there to be clothed with earthly matter.

Then comes the moment when we draw near to earthly life. We now feel the universe, which until recently was ours, vanishing from us. It shrinks and wanes, and this experience begets in us the longing to come down again to earth, once more to unite with a physical body on the earth. For the great universe we had before withdraws, eludes our spiritual gaze; now therefore do we look to become a human being again.

All this involves, however, quite another timescale. Life between death and rebirth goes on for many centuries, and if a human being is born, say, in the twentieth century his descent will have been prepared for gradually—even as early as the sixteenth century. All through this time he himself has, moreover, in a certain sense been working down into earthly conditions and events.

A distant great-grandfather of yours, way back in the sixteenth century, fell in love with a distant great-grandmother. They felt the urge to come together, and in this urge you were already at work from spiritual worlds. And in the seventeenth century, when a less distant great-grandfather and great-grandmother loved each other, you once again were in a sense the mediator. In this way you summoned all the generations to the end that at long last those should emerge who could become your mother and your father.

Forces are at work in that mysterious and intangible quality that pervades the relationships of earthly love which proceed from those looking for future incarnations. Therefore full consciousness and freedom are never there in the external conditions which bring men and women on earth together. These things still lie outside the range of human understanding.

1.6 The spread of esoteric truth and the future of reproduction

The only question now is: what are the ways and means by which humanity may attain spirituality, that is, the overcoming of materialism, and at the same time reach what may be called the bond of brotherhood, the expression of universal human love? One might imagine that universal human love need only be stressed strongly enough, and that then it must come about; or that one should found fraternities which aim at the goal of a universal human love. Spiritual science is never of this opinion. On the contrary! The more people speak of universal brotherly love and humanity, becoming in a sense intoxicated by these, the more egoistic they become. For like a lust of the senses there is also a lust of the soul. It is in fact a refined voluptuousness to say: I will become morally higher and higher. Although this thought does not lead to ordinary conventional egoism, it does lead to a subtle form of egoism arising from such voluptuousness.

It is not by emphasizing 'love' or 'sympathy' that these are generated in the course of human evolution. Humanity is much more likely to be led to that bond of brotherhood by something else, namely by spiritual knowledge itself. There is no other means of bringing about a universal human brotherhood than the spreading of esoteric knowledge through the world. One may talk for ever of Love and the Brotherhood of Mankind, one may found thousands of fraternities; they will not lead to the desired goal, however well-intentioned they may be. The point is to use the right means, to know how to found this bond of brotherhood and sisterhood. Only those whose lives are grounded in universal esoteric truth, valid for all human beings, find themselves together in the one truth. As the sun unites the plants which strive towards it while yet remaining individually separate, so must the truth to which all are striving be a uniform one; then all human beings will come together. But they must work energetically towards truth, for only then can they live together in harmony.

You might object that surely all are striving towards the truth, but that there are different standpoints, and therefore strife and dissensions arise. This denotes an insufficiently thorough knowledge of truth. One must not plead that there may be different standpoints; one must first experience that truth is single and indivisible. It does not depend on popular vote; it is true in itself. Or would you put it to the vote as to whether the three angles of a triangle add up to 180 degrees? Whether millions of people agree about this or not a single one, when you have recognized it, it is true for you. There is no democracy about truth. Those who are not yet in harmony have not penetrated far enough into the truth, and this is the origin of all dispute over truth. You might say: yes, but one person asserts this and another that in esoteric matters! In genuine esotericism that is not so. It is the same in esoteric things as in materialistic things; there, too, someone asserts this and another that, but then one of them is wrong. It is the same with genuine esotericism; but people often have a bad habit of judging esoteric matters before they have understood them.

The aim of the sixth epoch of humanity will be to popularize esoteric truth in the widest circles; that is the mission of that epoch. A society which is united in spirit has the task of carrying this esoteric truth everywhere—right into life—and applying it practically. This is precisely what is lacking in our age. Just look how our epoch is searching and how no one can find the right solution. There are innumerable problems, the education problem, women's suffrage, medicine, the social problem, the food question. People chip away at these problems, endless articles are written, and each talks from his or her own standpoint, without being willing to study the esoteric truth that lies at the centre.

Thus human beings themselves will bring about the future shape of their bodies. Inasmuch as they become softer and softer, inasmuch as they separate themselves from the hard part, they will be approaching their future. An age will come when they will live above their earthly part, as was the case in times gone by. This condition, which is comparable to your present sleep-condition, will then be replaced by another when the human being will be able to draw his etheric body out of his physical body at will. It will be as if the denser part were here below on earth while the human being makes use of it from outside like an instrument. Human beings will no longer carry their bodies about and live within them, but will float above them; the bodies themselves will have become rarefied and more delicate. This seems fantastic now, but one can be distinctly aware of it from spiritual laws, just as one can calculate future eclipses of the sun and moon from the laws of astronomy.

Above all it will be upon the reproductive force that the human being will work. He will transform it. Many people cannot imagine that there will ever be a different reproductive process. But it will be so; the process of reproduction will be altered. The reproductive process and all that is connected with it will pass in the future to another organ. The organ that is already preparing to become the future organ of reproduction is the human larynx. Today it can only bring forth vibrations of the air, can only impart to the air what lies in a word that goes forth from it, so that the vibrations correspond to the word. Later on, not only will the word press forward in its rhythm from the larynx, but it will be illuminated by the human being, it will be suffused by substance itself. Just as today the word only becomes air waves, so in the future the person's inner being, his own likeness, which today is in his word, will issue from the larynx. The human being will proceed from the human being, the human being will speak forth the human being. This in the future will be how a new human being is born—by being spoken forth by another.

Such things throw a specific light on phenomena in our surroundings which no ordinary science can explain. The transformation of reproduction, which will once again be non-sexual, will supersede the previous manner of reproduction. That is why in the male organism at the age of puberty a change also takes place in the larynx, making the voice deeper. This is a direct indication of how these two things are interconnected. Thus spiritual wisdom throws light again and again on facts of life and illumines phenomena for which materialistic science can give you no explanation.

2. Male and Female

In these extracts Rudolf Steiner goes more into the nature and attributes of male and female. With the rise of the women's movement in the 1960s, it was hotly debated as to whether men and women were intrinsically different in their soul or psychological make-up, or whether any differences were merely due to conditioning. The latter view seemed to gain the ground until more recently, when the popularity of books such as John Gray's Men Are From Mars and Women Are From Venus[17] *suggests otherwise. The first lecture is printed in entirety as it has only appeared before in an old journal, and reveals that much of the 'difference' is due to the fact that the etheric or life body contains the characteristics of the sex opposite to that of the physical body. This lies at the root of Jung's anima/animus concept. But importantly Rudolf Steiner shows how the truly spiritual part of the human being is beyond gender, which is like a sheath for it. Our gender provides us with different life experiences, so that in our successive earth lives we reappear as male and female alternately—or sometimes as having two or more incarnations as the same gender before switching. The next three extracts deal with child development at the stage of puberty when soul differences emerge more strongly with the physical changes. The difference in how men and women experience love will surely ring true for many readers.*

Differences in adolescent behaviour are as obvious today as when the lectures were given, such as the awkward silent boy and the coquettish self-displaying girl—the popularity of social networking websites cunningly feed into and enhance these characteristics. Steiner stresses the dangers of obsessive eroticism developing (which probably has become much stronger since his time) and recommends the development of an aesthetic sense as a counteracting force. Sadly our unaesthetic surroundings rarely encourage this. We can only wish Steiner's recommendations for working with adolescents were heeded more widely.

In the last two extracts Steiner addresses specifically the question of women in society as referred to in the introduction, but that ultimately we are all striving to be truly 'human'.

2.1 Man and woman in the light of spiritual science

Anthroposophical spiritual science does not exist in order that human beings be estranged from life through some kind of mysticism. It should in no way divert people from their tasks in daily life or the present. On the contrary, spiritual science should bring strength, energy and open mindedness to humanity so that people can meet what daily life and our times demand. Hence it follows that spiritual science must not concern itself solely with the great riddles of existence, of the nature of human existence and the meaning of the world, but must also seek to cast light on those questions which confront us directly. Therefore in these lectures we shall deal throughout with what are commonly called questions of our time.

But whoever would speak out of spiritual science on such contemporary issues finds himself in a special position, for he raises the expectation that he will directly enter these current debates. And this expectation arises very easily with regard to the question of man and woman, or man, woman and child. Yet precisely because the spiritual researcher must consider these questions from a higher vantage point his observations seem to lead away from the outlook and opinions arising in conventional discussions. Although spiritual science must indeed look at these questions from a higher perspective, it is precisely spiritual science which is able to work most practically on these issues. For while it is of the nature of spiritual-scientific observation that such questions are raised into their eternal context, at the same time such observation makes visible practical solutions to concrete problems (unlike party programmes, slogans and the like which prove to be unworkable in practice). This must always be remembered when considering the relationship of man and woman from a higher vantage point. Many of the things to be said will sound quite strange. But if you penetrate deeper into them you will discover that spiritual science can offer a far more thorough answer to questions of practical life than can be found in other quarters.

Spiritual science takes its start from the knowledge that behind all that is sense perceptible stands a soul-spiritual nature. Only when we turn our gaze towards the spiritual lying behind the sense world will the questions with which we wish to concern ourselves appear in their right light. And so we must ask ourselves: what is the spiritual nature of the two sexes? We shall then see that the truths revealed by spiritual science are already sensed by many today, even by those of a materialistic world outlook. But as these inklings are only based on a materialistic conception they often appear as illusory.

What then does materialism have to say about the nature of the sexes? We may best orientate ourselves towards this question by considering that women have for some time sought to approach the time in human evolution when both sexes shall attain full equality. In so far as women have stepped into the struggle for their rights, it is important for us to learn what materialism has to say about female nature.

Then we will find a point of reference on how the modern world thinks about this question. One could quote the most varying ideas on female nature such as they appear in the book *Zur Kritik der Weiblichkeit* (A Survey of the Woman Problem) by Rosa Mayreder.[18] It is indeed very good to seek the opinions of leading personalities of the day on issues of this kind.

A very noteworthy scientist of the nineteenth century described the basic quality of woman to be humility. Another whose comment is equally valid declared it to be an angry disposition. Another scientist who sparked off much controversy came to the conclusion that female nature is basically submissive, while yet another felt it consisted of the desire to dominate. One described women as conservative, still another felt women to be the true revolutionary element in the world. And yet another said that the ability to analyse was well developed in women, as opposed to others who believed that women lack this quality entirely and have only developed the capacity for synthesis.

This quaint collection could be extended indefinitely, though in the end one would only learn that through looking at things on a purely external level intelligent people are led to opposite conclusions. Those who wish to enter into the thing more deeply must ask whether perhaps these observers are starting from false premises. One cannot merely look at externalities, rather one must consider the whole being of the human being. An inkling of the truth dawned in many researchers through the facts themselves. However this was submerged by materialistic thought. For example a young man, Otto Weininger, wrote a book entitled *Geschlecht und Charakter* (Sex and Character).[19] Otto Weininger was a man with great potential which, however, he was unable to develop because the full weight of materialism rested heavily on his soul. He was of the opinion that the individual human being can be seen neither as entirely masculine nor feminine but rather that the masculine is mixed together with the feminine and vice versa. This embryo of an idea dawned in the soul of Weininger but was stultified by the prevailing materialism. Thus Weininger imagined there to be a mixing and material interaction of the masculine and feminine principles such that in every man a hidden woman and in every woman a hidden man is to be found. But he drew some strange conclusions from this. Weininger said for example that the woman possesses no ego, individuality, character or personality, no freedom and so on. As his theory was concerned only with a purely material, quantitative mixing of male and female properties it followed that the man possesses all of these things. These, however, came to nothing in him because of his other male qualities. Thus if we enter into this logically we soon discover a theory which destroys itself. Yet as we shall see, there is some truth in it.

I have emphasized again and again that it is not as easy to understand the human being on the basis of spiritual science as it is on the basis of a materialistically orientated science. For that which we perceive as the sense-perceptible human being is for spiritual science only one component of the whole being, namely the physical body. Beyond that, however, spiritual science distinguishes the etheric body which the human has in common with animals and plants. As a third component of the human being it characterizes the astral or soul body as that which lives in our feelings and sensations and is the bearer of our joys and sorrows. This component we have in common with the animal world. And as the fourth component spiritual science recognizes that which makes human beings human and conscious of themselves—the ego. Spiritual science thus describes the human being as possessing four components.

At present we will concern ourselves with the physical and etheric bodies. For herein lies the solution to the riddle of the sexes. The etheric body is only to a certain extent a picture of the physical body. In regard to the sexes things are different. In the man the etheric body is female and in the woman it is male. However strange it may seem, a deeper observation will disclose the following: something of the opposite sex lies hidden in each person. It is no good however to look for all kinds of abnormal phenomena; rather one needs to pay attention to normal experiences. By confronting this fact, it is no longer possible in the strict sense to speak of man and woman, but rather of masculine and feminine qualities. Certain qualities in the woman work more outwardly while others are more inward. The woman has masculine qualities within herself and the man feminine qualities. For example a man becomes a warrior through the outer courage of his bodily nature, a woman possesses an inner courage, the courage of sacrifice and devotion. The man brings his creative activity to bear on external life. The woman works with devoted receptivity into the world. Countless phenomena in life will become clear to us if we think of human nature as the working together of two polar opposites. In the man the masculine pole works outwards and the feminine lives more inwardly, while in the woman the opposite holds true.

Spiritual science however also shows us a deeper reason why a masculine quality is to be found in the woman and a feminine in the man. Spiritual science speaks of how human beings strive after ever greater perfection, through many lives. Our present life is always the result of a previous one.

Thus as we proceed through many lives, we experience both male and female incarnations. What arises in this way may be expressed as the effect of those experiences gathered on both sides in earthly life.

Whoever is able in this way to look more deeply into the male and female natures knows that the more intimate experiences of the two sexes are very different, and must be very different. Our entire earth existence is a collection of the most varied experiences. However, these experiences can only become comprehensive through their being acquired from the viewpoint of both sexes. Hence we can see that even if we only consider the human being with regard to the two lower members, we see in reality a being with two sides. So long as one merely looks at the physical body little can be understood. The spiritual lying behind must also be recognized. Through his masculine nature the inner femininity of the man appears, and through the woman's feminine nature her inner masculinity appears. Now one can grasp why it is that so many misjudgements have been made about this question; it depends on whether one looks at the inner or the outer aspects. In considering only one side of the human being, one is subjected entirely to chance. If, for example, one researcher finds that the main quality of the woman is humility and another that it is an angry disposition, it simply means that both have observed only one side of the same being. Error must occur with this kind of approach. In order to recognize the full truth we must look at the whole human being.

Something else must also be taken into account in order to gain knowledge of the whole truth. We must observe the human being in alternating sleeping and waking states. During sleep the astral body and the ego are raised out of the physical-etheric organism of the human being. On falling asleep one loses one's day consciousness; one enters into a different state of consciousness—a sleep consciousness. The perceptions and experiences that are made by the ego and astral body during sleep in the spiritual world remain hidden to our usual consciousness. In the present evolutionary state the human being is organized in such a way that the ego and astral bodies must make use of the physical sense organs in order to become aware of the physical world. That we see, hear, taste, and so on with our physical organs of sense is an idea widely held today. A thinker like Fichte,[20] however, would say: the ear does not hear—I hear. The ego, the human being's true inner being, is therefore the starting point for all our sense perceptions. And each morning when we awaken, the ego and astral body experience new knowledge of the physical world through the sense organs. It is different during sleep, for the ego and astral body spend their time in the spiritual world. The human being has sense organs in the astral body which enable perception in the astral world, but these have normally not been developed. Those who are unable to accept this as a possibility would have to say that in reality human beings die every evening, if they are to be consistent. But human beings do find themselves in the spiritual world at night.

Further than this, the spiritual and physical worlds have a unique relationship to one another, for everything physical is only a very dense form of the spiritual. In the same way as ice is densified water, so are the physical and etheric bodies a densification of the astral body. Present-day materialism will find it very hard to admit that the spirit creates everything material. It is, however, the tragedy of materialism that it understands the nature of matter least of all. One arrives at some very strange conclusions if one denies that matter is a condensed form of the spiritual. Naturally if one stays with popular concepts, most people will not immediately recognize anything less than pure reason in such a sentence as the following: 'The body is the foundation for our true soul nature; all so-called spiritual things can be guided through that which is bodily.' It becomes much clearer, however, if one takes it to its logical conclusion, as is done for instance in that pragmatism which comes from America. One single sentence will easily show how this theory speaks pure nonsense to the human mind. Thus it declares that man does not cry because he is sad, but rather is sad because he cries. That a soul mood might have an effect on the physical is not deemed possible; instead one believes that some outside event causes the tears to run which then makes the person sad. This is the consequence of materialism carried to its logical absurdity.

Spiritual science knows that the two higher members of the human being, the ego and the astral body, leave during the night while the physical and etheric bodies remain behind. Thus it follows that during sleep the human being leaves behind male and female aspects and lives as a sexually undifferentiated being in the spiritual world. Everyone's life is thus divided between a sexual and an asexual experience.

Do the sexes then have no meaning in the spiritual world? Does the polarity of physical and etheric body, which makes the two sexes manifest here on earth, find no echo in the higher worlds? Certainly we do not take our sexual nature with us into higher worlds; however, the origin of the two sexes is to be found in the astral sphere. In the same way as ice is formed from water, that which meets us in the physical world as masculine and feminine is formed out of the polarity of higher principles. We can approach this best if we consider it as the polarity of life and form. This polarity is also expressed in nature. We can see budding life in the tree and at the same time that which builds up hard forms, slows down growth and transforms it into the solid trunk. Life and form must work together in everything that lives. And if we look at the nature of the sexes from this standpoint we can say: that which corresponds to the life principle is the masculine, while that which brings life into a certain form expresses itself in the feminine. That which an artist creates in the way of form in marble, for example, is not to be found in outer nature. Only the artist's inner being, which is rooted in the spiritual world and finds its nourishment there, can be artistically creative. Indeed the reality is that the forces and beings of the spiritual world are continually streaming into the astral body and ego of the human being. And that which the artist creates as an imprint on matter is a memory of something with which he has been stimulated in the spiritual world. Were the human being unable to return to a spiritual homeland during sleep, it would not be possible to carry into physical existence the seeds needed to initiate great and noble deeds. Therefore nothing could be worse for the human being than prolonged loss of sleep.

That which the artist has drawn from the spiritual world and has built unconsciously into his work then appears as life and form. One might ask why it is that the Juno Ludovisi[21] appears so wonderful to us. There is the large face, the wide forehead, the unusual nose. If we try and feel our way into this image we would come to experience how impossible it is to think away the spiritual; soul and spirit are to be found in the very form of this face. This form could stay like this forever. The inner life has become entirely form, is fixed in form; soul and spirit have become form. But then we look up at the head of Zeus. Soul and spirit are present in this rather narrow forehead too, but one has the feeling that this form could change at any moment. Out of a deep inspiration the artist has been able to hold on to life and form in all its reality.

But just as the artist is able to mould life and form into his great works, so is our whole being in reality life and form. This in itself shows that human nature is of spiritual origin and is created out of life, out of the continuous process of life and that which gives it permanence. The human being experiences life and death as the expression of this higher polarity of existence. It is in this sense that Goethe could say: 'Death is the means by which nature can create more life.' Thus life finds a form not for one-sided life, nor one-sided death, but for a higher harmonious whole which can be created through life and death together. On this basis spiritual and physical can work together through the medium of masculine and feminine; the eternally developing life in the masculine, and life held in form in the feminine principle.

When investigating the nature of the sexes we have not begun with a one-sided observation of physical existence but rather have sought an answer on the spiritual level of existence. The harmony above the sexes can only be found in so far as the two sexes raise themselves to that level. If, therefore, by making use of the knowledge to be gained from spiritual science we could enable the reality beyond the sexes to take effect in practical life, the problem of the sexes would be solved. This does not lead away from life however. For that which meets us in the two phenomena of human nature can best be clarified by consciously striving for this higher harmony. In this way the question of the sexes will be deepened and the polarities will be harmonized. Everything in the nature of the sexes attains a very different form and meaning. We cannot solve this question through dogma, rather we must seek a common ground, and find perceptions and feelings which lead beyond the sexes. The question regarding the sexes will be solved in direct social interaction in such as way as is appropriate for advanced humanity. Once human beings find that which transcends the sexes, then this issue of our time will have been resolved.

These observations have shown, as is found again and again, that we must distinguish between the reality of the senses and the nature of being itself. If we want to solve the riddles of life, we must observe the whole human being from the world of the senses and from the world of the spirit. It can be seen that beyond the sense-perceptible polarity man and woman are only garments, sheaths which hide the true nature of the human being. We must search behind the garments, for there is the spirit. We must not merely consider the outer side of the spirit; we must enter into the spirit itself.

We could also express it in this way: Love saturated with wisdom or wisdom penetrated with love is the highest goal. 'The eternal feminine draws us forward.'[22] The feminine is that element in the world which strives outward in order to be fertilized by the eternal elements of life.

2.2 Puberty and adolescence and the difference between men and women

And now, what actually happens when sexual maturity occurs? Our considerations of the last few days have already shed some light on it. We have seen how, after the change of teeth, the child is still working inwardly with those forces which, to a certain degree, have become emancipated soul and spiritual forces. During the subsequent stages the child incarnates via the respiratory system and blood circulation to where in the tendons the muscles grow onto the bones. It incarnates from within outwards towards the human periphery, and at the time of sexual maturity the young adolescent breaks through into the external world. Only then does she or he fully stand in the world.

This makes it imperative for us to approach the adolescent who has passed through sexual maturity quite differently from the way in which we dealt with him or her prior to this event. For, fundamentally, the previous processes involving the emancipated soul and spiritual forces before puberty had as yet nothing to do with sex in its own realm. True, boys and girls show a definite predisposition towards their sexes, but this cannot be considered as actual sexuality. Sexuality only develops after the breakthrough into the external world, when a new relationship with the outer world has been established.

But then, at this particular time, something is happening within the realm of the adolescent's soul and bodily nature, which is not unlike what happened previously during the second dentition. During the change of teeth, forces were liberated to become actively engaged in the child's thinking, feeling and willing forces which were directed more towards the memory. The powers of memory were then released. Now, at puberty, something else becomes available for free activity in the soul realm. These are powers which previously had entered the rhythms of breathing and which subsequently were striving to introduce rhythmical qualities also into the muscular and even into the skeletal system. This rhythmical element now becomes transmuted into the adolescent's receptiveness for all that belongs to the realm of creative ideas, for all that belongs to the imagination. Fundamentally speaking, genuine powers of imagination only come to birth during puberty, for they can come into their own only after the astral body has been born. It is this same astral body which exists beyond time and space and which links together past, present and future according to its own principles, as we can experience it in our dreams.

What is it that the adolescent brings with him when he 'breaks through' into the external world via his skeletal system? It is what he originally brought down with him from pre-earthly existence and what, gradually, has become interwoven with his whole inner being. And now, with the onset of sexual maturity, the adolescent is being cast out of the spiritual world, as it were. Without exaggerating, one can really put it that strongly, for it represents the actual truth; with the onset of puberty the young human being is cast out from the living world of the spirit, and thrown into the external world which he or she can perceive only by means of the physical and etheric body. And though the adolescent is not at all aware of what is going on inside him, subconsciously this plays an all the more intensive part. Subconsciously, or semi-consciously, it makes the adolescent compare the world he has now entered with the world which he formerly had within himself. Previously, he had not experienced the spiritual world consciously but, nevertheless, he had found it possible to live in harmony with it. His inner being felt attuned to it and ready to work freely with the soul and spiritual realm. But now, in these changed conditions, the external world no longer offers such possibilities to him. It presents all kinds of hindrances which, in themselves, create the wish to overcome them. This, in turn, gives rise to the tumultuous relationship between the adolescent and the surrounding world, lasting from the fourteenth or fifteenth year till the early twenties.

This inner upheaval is bound to come and it is well for us to be aware of it already during the preceding years. There may be people of an unduly sensitive nature who believe that it would be better to save teenagers from such inner turmoil, only to find that they have made themselves their greatest enemy. It would be quite wrong to try to spare them this tempestuous time of life. It is far better to plan ahead in one's educational aims so that what has been done with the pre-puberty child can now come to the help and support of the adolescent's soul and spiritual struggles.

We must be clear that with the arrival of puberty an altogether different being emerges, born out of a new relationship with the world. It is no good appealing to the adolescent's previous respect for authority, for now he demands to know reasons for whatever he is expected to do. We must get into the habit of approaching the young man or woman rationally. For example, if the adolescent who has been led by the spiritual world into this earthly world becomes rebellious because this new world is so different from what he had expected, the adult must try to show him— and this without any pedantry—that everything he meets in the world has arisen from what has gone before, from history. One must act the part of the expert who really understands why things have come to be as they are. From now on, one will accomplish nothing by way of authority. Now one has to be able to convince the adolescent through the sheer weight of one's indisputable knowledge and expertise and by giving him watertight reasons for everything one does or expects of him. If, at this stage, the pupil cannot see sound reasons in all the content given to him, if conditions in the world appear to make no sense to him, he will begin to doubt the rightness of his previous life. He will feel himself in opposition with what he had experienced during those years which, apparently, only led him into these present unacceptable outer conditions. And if, during his inner turmoil, he cannot find contact with people who are able to reassure him, at least to a certain extent, that there are good reasons for what is happening in the world, then the inner stress may become intolerable to the extent that the adolescent breaks down altogether. For this newly emerged astral body is not of this world. The young person has been cast out of the astral world and he is willing to place himself into this earthly world only if he feels convinced of its rightful existence.

You will completely misunderstand what I have been describing if you think that the adolescent is at all aware of what is thus going on within him. During his ordinary day-consciousness it rises up from the unconscious in dim feelings. It is surging up through blunted will impulses. It lives itself out in the disappointment of apparently unattainable ideals, in frustrated desires and perhaps also in a certain inner dullness towards what presents itself out there in the unreasonable happenings of the world.

If, during this stage, education is to be effective at all—and this indeed must be the case for any youngster willing to learn—then the teaching content must be transmitted in the appropriate form. It must also be a preparation for the years to come, up to the early twenties or even later in life. Having suffered the wounds inflicted by life and having paid back in his own coinage, the young person of 15 to 21 or 22 eventually will have to find his way back again into the world from which he had been cast out during puberty. The duration of this period varies, especially so during our chaotic times which tend to prolong it even further into adult life. The young person must feel accepted again; he must be able to make a new contact with the spiritual world, for without it life is not possible. However, should he feel any coercion coming from those in authority, this new link will lose all meaning and value for life.

If we are aware of these difficulties already well before the arrival of puberty, we will make good use of the child's inborn longing for authority in order to bring it to the stage when there is no longer any need for an authoritarian approach. And this stage should coincide with the coming of sexual maturity. But by then the educator must always be ready and able to give convincing reasons for everything he wishes his pupil to do.

Seen from a wider, spiritual perspective, we can thus observe the grandiose metamorphosis which is taking place in the human being during the period of sexual maturity.

It is of the greatest importance to realize that the whole question of sex becomes a reality only during puberty, when the adolescent enters the external world in the way I have described. Naturally, since everything in life is relative, this, too, has to be taken as a relative truth. Nevertheless, one has to recognize that up to the stage of sexual maturity the child lives more as a general human being and that an experience of the world differentiated according to whether one lives as a man or woman only begins with the onset of puberty. This realization—which in our generally intellectual and naturalistic civilization cannot be taken for granted—will allow people who, without prejudice, are striving for a knowledge of the human being, a real insight into the relationship between the sexes. It also helps them to understand the problem regarding the position of women in society, not only during our present times but also in the future.

Only if one can appreciate the tremendous metamorphosis that is taking place in the male organism during voice mutation—to mention just one example—will one be able to understand fully the statement that up to the age of sexual maturity the child retains a more general human character, as yet undivided into sexes. Other similar processes occur also in the female organism, only in a different area. The human voice with its ability to moderate and to form sounds and tones, is a manifestation of the human being's general human nature. It is born out of the soul and spiritual substance which is working upon the child up to puberty. Changes of pitch and register, on the other hand, occurring during mutation are the result of external influences. They are forced upon the adolescent from outside, as it were. They are the means by which he places himself into the outer world with his innermost being. It is not only a case of the soft parts in the larynx relating themselves more strongly to the bones, but a slight ossification of the larynx itself takes place which fundamentally amounts to a withdrawal of the larynx from the purely human inner nature into a more earthly existence.

This stepping out into the world should really be seen in a much wider context than is usually the case. Usually, in people's minds, the capacity to love which awakens at this time is directly linked to sexual attraction. But this is by no means the whole story. The power to love, born during sexual maturity, embraces everything within the adolescent's entire compass. Love between the sexes is but one specific and limited aspect of love in the world. Only by seeing human love in this light can one understand it correctly, and then one also understands its task in the world.

What is really happening in a human being during the process of sexual maturity? Prior to this stage, as a child, his relationship to the world was one where he could imitate the surroundings and be subject to its authority. Outer influences were working upon him, for at that time his inner being mainly represented what he had brought down with him from pre-earthly life. Humanity as a whole had to work upon him from without, first through the principle of imitation and then through authority. But now, at puberty, having found his own way into humanity and no longer depending on its outer support to the same extent that a pre-pubescent child does, there rises up in him a new feeling, an entirely new appraisal of humankind as a whole. It is this new experience of humankind which represents the spiritual counterpart to the physical faculty of reproduction. Physically he becomes able to procreate. Spiritually he becomes capable of experiencing humankind as a totality.

During this new stage, the polarity between man and woman becomes very marked. Only through a real understanding of the other sex by means of social intercourse, also in the realm of soul and spirit, is it possible for the human potential to come to some kind of realization on earth. Both man and woman fully represent humankind, but each in a differentiated way. The woman sees in humanity a gift of the metaphysical worlds. Fundamentally, she sees humanity as the result of a divine outpouring. Unconsciously and in the depths of her soul she bears a picture of humankind which acts as her standard, and she evaluates and assesses mankind according to this standard. If these remarks are not generally accepted today, it is due to the fact that our present civilization shows all the signs of a male-dominated society.

For a long period of time the most powerful influences in our civilization have displayed a decidedly masculine character. An example of this—however grotesque it may sound—can be found in Freemasonry. It is symbolic of our times that men, if they wish to keep certain matters to themselves, separate themselves off into Lodges of Freemasonry. There are also Lodges in which both men and women congregate but in these Freemasonry has already become blunted, they no longer bear its original stamp. The constitution of Freemasonry is of course a specific example, but it is nevertheless indicative of the male-dominated character of our society. Women, too, have absorbed a great deal of the masculine element in our civilization and because of this they are actually preventing the specifically feminine element from coming into its own. This is the reason why one so often gains the impression that with regard to inner substance and outer form there is hardly any difference between the ideals and programmes of the various women's movements and those of men, even to the very tone of speeches in which they are delivered. Obviously these movements are different from each other in so far as on the one side demands are made to safeguard women's interests, while on the other they are made on behalf of men. But with regard to inner substance, they are scarcely distinguishable from each other.

Man, in his innermost being, experiences humanity as something of an enigma. To him it appears as something unfathomable which poses endless questions, the solutions of which seem to lie beyond his powers. This typically masculine characteristic expresses itself in all the mysterious ceremonial with its dry and manly atmosphere which belongs to Freemasonry. This same male tendency has permeated our culture to such an extent that, on the one hand, the women are suffering under it and, on the other, they are wanting to emulate it, wishing to make it part of their lives, too.

If you take a good look at modern medicine with all its materialistic features, if you see how it fails to comprehend human nature, especially with regard to its physical aspect, so that it depends on experimentation—if you observe modern medicine, you will find there the product of a distinctly masculine attitude, however strange this may sound to you. In fact, one could hardly find a better illustration of male thinking than in what modern medicine so blatantly reveals to us.

If one deals with the truth today, people tend to think that one does so merely for the sake of putting paradoxical statements into the world. Yet the reality is often paradoxical. Therefore if one wishes to speak the truth, one has to put up with appearing paradoxical, however inconvenient this may be.

While womankind lives more in the image it creates of humanity, man's experiences of humanity are more of a wishful and enigmatic kind. In order to understand this situation, one needs to become clear about one other symptom of our times, which is of particular significance for the art of teaching: when people speak about love today, they do not generally differentiate between the various kinds of love. Of course, one can generalize the concept of love, just as one can speak about condiments in a general way. But if someone puts abstract speculations about certain matters into the world and then holds forth about them, it always strikes me as if he were talking about salt, sugar or pepper merely in terms of condiments. He only needs to apply such abstractions to practical life by putting salt into his coffee instead of sugar—because, after all, both are condiments—to realize his foolishness. Anyone who indulges in general speculations instead of entering the concrete realities of life, commits the same folly.

A woman's love is very different from that of a man. Her love originates in the imaginative realm and it is constantly engaged in creating an image. A woman does not love a man just as he is, standing there before her in ordinary humdrum life—forgive me for saying this but, after all, men are not exactly of the kind a healthy imagination could fall in love with—but she weaves into her love the ideal she has received as heaven's gift. Man's love, on the other hand, is tinged with desire; it is of a wishful nature. This differentiation needs to be made, no matter whether it shows itself more in an idealistic or a realistic sense. Ideal love may inspire longings of an ideal nature. The instinctive and sensuous kind may be a mere product of fancy. But this fundamental difference between love as it lives in a man or a woman is a reality. A woman's love is steeped in imagination. In man's love there is an element of desire. It is just because of this complementary character that the two kinds of love can become harmonized in life.

An educator should bear this in mind when confronted with pupils who have already passed through the stage of sexual maturity. He should realize that by that time it is no longer possible to bring to them certain things which belong to the pre-adolescent stage, and that the opportunity for doing so has been missed. Therefore, in order to prevent a one-sided attitude in later life, one must endeavour to give to pre-pubescent children enough of the right content to last them through the coming stages.

In our times when, fortunately, coeducation in both primary and secondary education is accepted more and more readily so that boys and girls work side by side in order to learn how to cooperate as men and women in social life later on, it is of special importance to pay heed to what has just been said. Through it, a contemporary phenomenon such as the women's movement will be placed upon a really sound and healthy basis.

2.3 *Differences in educating boys and girls during adolescence*

At the time of the change of teeth, when the child reaches school age, we are confronted with a situation in which a completely objective event takes place in the external physical body of the child, that is to say, in that part of him which every night when he enters into the state of sleep separates itself off as something quite objective that is left behind. When puberty is reached, however, the human being brings his whole subjective nature—ego and astral body—into relationship with his objective nature—etheric body and physical body.

Consequently the transition with which we have to deal here intervenes in the soul's development in a way that is altogether different from what we can observe at the time of the change of teeth. There a union of physical and etheric was taking place which then also had its effect upon the subjective nature. Here the physical-etheric remains as it is and the astral also, together with the ego, remains as it is. What happens is that a new kind of intercourse begins to arise between physical-etheric on the one hand and astral-ego on the other, with the result that both take equal share in the transition. For in reaching puberty, the inner subjective attributes of the human being are also directly involved.

Hence those marked changes in character which can be observed in a boy or girl who has reached the age of puberty.

These changes in character are indeed quite perceptible outwardly. We notice what I may call a maturity with regard to love which does not at first show itself in its full sexual form but in a more general way. One child begins to feel inwardly drawn to another. In particular we can see friendships developing in this way between boys and girls, where, to begin with, sex plays but a small part. Such friendships are however evidence of the unfolding of the power to love; they show us that the force of attraction between human beings is beginning to enter more consciously into the development of the boy or girl.

And then we begin to detect in both boys and girls of this age something that is not easily accounted for from their development so far, is indeed quite often in sharp contrast to the character they have shown in earlier childhood. At the same time we can observe a widening of human interests; the new development shows something of a universal quality. We sometimes call it in boys the awkward age; in girls it takes a rather different form. As a matter of fact, all its symptoms are due to the specific inner experience that the astral body encounters at this time—and with it also the ego, though the latter has, of course, not yet come to full development. The astral body is trying to relate itself in the right way to the experiences that are being undergone by the physical system, and thereby to the whole surrounding world. This search for a right relationship between subjective and objective gives rise to a kind of struggle in the human being which accounts for the contradiction that children of this age often present. For you will, in fact, sometimes hardly recognize children again when they have entered this stage.

The external characteristics of this awkward stage in boys and girls are familiar to all, and there is no need for me to give any detailed description of them. What we must do, however, is to enter upon a careful study of these characteristics and get to know their real nature; we shall find it to be a study of immense importance for education.

The first thing to be noticed is that the astral body has more significance in girls than it has in boys. This holds true throughout life; and because of it, the female organism has a stronger inclination towards the cosmos. Many secrets of the cosmos reveal themselves in the female organism. The astral body of the woman is more highly differentiated, more delicately organized than the astral body of the man. We may even say that the latter is crude in comparison.

On the other hand, the ego of a girl between the ages of 13 or 14 and 20 or 21 is more strongly under the influence of the developments that are going on in her astral body. One can see through these years the ego being gradually absorbed by the astral body until at length, at the age of 20 or 21, a reaction takes place and the girl makes a supreme effort to come to her own I, to attain egohood.

With boys it is essentially different. Their astral body does not draw in the ego to nearly so great an extent. The ego is still in concealment, it is not as yet properly active, and remains throughout these years very little influenced by the astral body. Just because the ego remains unabsorbed, while at the same time not yet independent, the boy may rather more easily than the girl not stand up for much. Girls of this age will often acquire a kind of freedom of manner, they will be more ready to come forward; whereas in boys, and especially in boys of deep feeling, more of an inclination to draw back is noticeable. This is due to the particular relation between ego and astral body that obtains in boys during the years of adolescence.

Boys will certainly make friends; but there is nevertheless in boys this need to be able to withdraw into themselves, where they can be with their own thoughts and feelings. Withdrawal into themselves is especially characteristic of boys who have rather deeper natures. The teacher (whether man or woman) can have a very good influence on a boy of this kind by responding in a delicate manner to what I may call the secret that every such boy conceals in his soul, by not nudging it too strongly but responding to it in a certain way and showing by his whole demeanour that he is aware of its existence. For in a boy of this age there is already something of a deep inclination to retire into himself.

Indeed if a boy does not show such signs of reserve, that should put us on our guard. Boys who do not show the slightest inclination to draw back into themselves in this way—and a good teacher will quickly observe it—need careful watching. The teacher must say to himself: I must look into this; something or other is not in order in the boy and might lead to difficulties, or even abnormalities, in later life.

On the other hand, in the girl we have quite a different situation. We are dealing here with rather fine and subtle traits of human nature, and one has to acquire a certain gift of observation to detect and distinguish them. The girl's ego is more or less absorbed—sucked up—by the astral. On this account the girl lives less within herself. For the ego-permeated astral body makes its way into the etheric body, enters deeply into it, and consequently into the whole demeanour of the girl, into her very movements and gestures. And we do in fact find that where girls are undergoing right and normal development they are ready at this age to take a stand in life; there is a certain sureness and confidence in the way they come forward and seek recognition. No drawing back into themselves!

To face the world frankly and freely is the natural attitude for a girl at this time of life. It may be coupled with rather egotistical feelings but it normally develops into an honest desire to make herself felt in the world, to give expression there to her own individual character. We must recognize that for girls to have this free carriage and to feel the importance of showing what they are worth is absolutely characteristic; it is in accord with their true and proper nature. In an extreme case, it leads to coquetry and vanity; the girl is not content with expressing herself in her soul qualities but wants also to make use of dress and outward appearance as a means of self-expression. It is very interesting to observe how, from the fourteenth or fifteenth year on, an aesthetic feeling for such things will generally show itself in girls. A more frivolous girl may develop at this age a quite inordinate love of finery.

All these manifestations are ultimately due to the fact that the astral body with the ego, which has been drawn into it, has entered into a special relationship with the etheric body. The relationship of astral to etheric comes out in the girl's walk and bearing, the way she carries her head more freely, disdainful in extreme cases and so on. We should certainly try to observe such things with something of an artistic eye.

As we begin to get a clear conception of the differences between boys and girls, we shall understand what good results can accrue from our work when we have the good fortune to teach them together. With tactful handling, a great deal can be achieved with a mixed class. The teacher who is conscious of the task he has undertaken will, when dealing with boys and girls together, nevertheless differentiate between them in certain respects. He will, for example, need to do so even in the matter of the relationship of the subjective nature to the external world. For we have now the task of bringing the subjective nature into a right relation with the child's own body, his etheric body and his physical body; and this requires that we shall have already succeeded in developing in him a right relationship to the external world. We must have this end in view right through the earlier years of school life. What proves to be so particularly important at the age of puberty must be our concern all the way up the school.

The teacher must, in the first place, see that the children receive impressions that are of a moral or religious kind. This has frequently been discussed among us. And then the children should also be receiving artistic impressions, artistic ideas. They should be led to appreciate beauty in the world, to look at the world from an aesthetic point of view. When the children reach their thirteenth, fourteenth or fifteenth year, we discover then how important it is that they should bring with them from their earlier school years feelings and ideas of this kind.

If a child has not had the feeling for beauty awakened in him, has not been educated to see the world from an aesthetic point of view, then that boy or girl will at this age of life tend to become sensual, perhaps even erotic. There is no better way of restraining eroticism than by a healthy development of the aesthetic sense, a feeling for what is noble and beautiful in nature. When you lead children to feel the beauty and the glory of sunrise and sunset, to be sensitive to the beauty of flowers and to the majesty of thunder and lightning, when, in short, you develop in them the aesthetic sense, you are doing far more for them than if you were to give them the sex education which it has now become customary to give to children at the earliest age and which is often carried to absurd lengths. A feeling for beauty, an aesthetic approach to the world—these are the things that restrain eroticism within its proper limits. As a child learns to perceive the world in all its beauty, he learns also to stand as a free being over against his own body; he is not oppressed by it. And that is what eroticism is—to be oppressed and tormented by one's own body.

Nor is it any less important that by this age the children should have developed certain moral and religious feelings. Such feelings always have a strengthening effect upon astral body and ego. These grow weak if there has been little development of moral and religious impulses. The child grows lethargic, as if physically paralysed. And this will show itself particularly at the age with which we are dealing. Lack of moral and religious impulse will come to expression in irregularity in the sexual life.

In all this preparation for the age of puberty we have to take account also of the differences between boys and girls. For the girl, the moral and ethical impressions we give her should incline to the aesthetic. We must do our best to present the moral, the good and the religious side of life so as to make them attractive, so that the girl feels them to be beautiful. She should feel joy in the knowledge that the whole world is permeated with the supersensory; her imagination should be richly supplied with pictures that are expressive of the divine that fills the world, expressive also of the beauty that reveals itself in the human being when he is good.

For the boy, on the other hand, it is the power that is at work in religion and morality that we must have more in mind. The girl needs to look at the religious and moral and see its beauty. With the boy we have rather to stress the courage and the sense of power that radiate from them. We must not of course push this to extremes, imagining we are to train girls to become so aesthetic as to see everything in that light alone, and boys to become bullies, as they would if we were to excite their egotism by appealing on all occasions to a feeling of power. We do right to arouse in the boy a sense of his own power, but it must be in association with things that are good and beautiful, and religious in the true sense.

We have to be careful to avoid letting the girls become superficial, mere spurious devotees of beauty in the awkward years; and with the boys we must take care that they do not develop into young hooligans. These are the dangers that threaten from both sides, as it were. And we need to be fully conscious of them, even while the children are still in the younger classes. We should lead the girls to find pleasure in what is good in the world, and to feel the beauty of what belongs to true religion. To the boys we should make a rather different appeal. We should constantly be telling them: 'See, if you do this, your muscles will grow taut, and you will be a fine, strong lad!' It is in such ways that a boy can be roused to a sense of the presence of the divine within him.

Now you must understand that these qualities that show themselves in boy and girl are deeply—but at the same time very delicately—embedded in their nature. Observation of the girl reveals that the ego is being absorbed by the astral body. I describe the situation in rather radical and extreme terms; it will however enable you to form a good picture of what is taking place. A process is going on in the soul and spirit that can be compared with the physical process of blushing. The whole development of a girl in this age of life may be called a blushing of soul and spirit; the penetration of the ego into the astral body is, in effect, a kind of blushing.

The situation is different in the boy. The ego is here less active, less lively. But it is not absorbed by the astral, with the result that we find in the boy a pallor of soul and spirit. This is quite noticeable, and is always present.

We must not allow ourselves to be deceived in this matter by physical appearance. If a girl becomes anaemic, then that is absolutely consistent with the fact that she blushes in soul and spirit. A boy may be a young rascal and readily over-excited, but that does not prevent his turning pale in soul and spirit. The conditions we find in boy and in girl are in reality both of them traceable to a kind of bashfulness, which takes possession of the whole human being at this time of life. It arises from the perception that he or she has now to receive into his or her own individual life something which must be kept secret and not revealed to the world. This accounts for the feeling of bashfulness, which enters right into regions of the soul that are the very most unconscious of all.

If we as teachers have the feeling that we must treat such things with respect, keeping the knowledge of them to ourselves, and dealing with the boys and girls with tact and delicacy, that will have its effect. No need for words: what tells here is the unspoken influence of one human being on another as we move about among the children, conscious of the presence within them of something they are anxious to watch over and cherish as one would an unopened flower-bud. If this feeling of respect and consideration is there in the teacher, then its very presence will have an immense educational influence.

It is really quite remarkable how the external symptoms that show themselves in a child of this age are all traceable to this sense of bashfulness, which is often however modified in such a way as to be turned almost into its opposite. The girl who is blushing in soul and spirit, and concealing her true being, puts herself forward, faces the world. But that is what is so strange in humankind altogether, that we manifest externally the very opposite of what is at work within. The bold and vigorous demeanour, drawing attention to herself, not putting up with things, the demand: 'I must be treated properly!' Anyone who has taught in a girls' boarding school will know how the girls carry on: they won't put up with that, they must be fairly treated. They are now emancipated, they will let him know what's what. They have their own thoughts; and are not going to be treated in that way. All this is really nothing but the reverse side of a kind of bashfulness which lives deep down in their soul, but of which they are as yet quite unconscious.

And then again with boys you will find the same. The awkwardness of the earlier years of adolescence and the more surly churlishness of the later, all the rather rough and rude behaviour that we meet with so often in boys in their teens, is once again nothing but evidence of a deep desire not to bring out into the open what they really are. What a boy does want is to make contact with the external world; and in his effort to do so he grows terribly clumsy in his movements, he is all over the place. We on our part however must never forget that all this irregular behaviour is only a sign that the boy is not showing us what he really is. In point of fact, the boy is, at this age of life, an imitator. In the first seven years of his life he was a natural, involuntary imitator; now he sets out purposely to imitate, first one person, then another. He is ever so pleased if he can make a good impression by imitating someone else's manner or action. He will try to walk like someone else. He will model his way of speaking on the speaking of another. He will copy even the rudeness of another, or again, try to be as refined and courteous as some other. In all this we have to see an endeavour to connect himself with the world. He is reluctant to lay bare his real self before the world, he would like to keep that back; consequently he appears quite different from what he really is.

Now the very worst thing that can happen here is that the teacher is lacking in humour. In dealing with boys of this age you simply must have humour, the kind of humour, let me say, that will lead you to respond to a situation but at the same time let the boy see that you do not really take it very seriously. You will need of course to have yourself well in hand if you are going to develop these two aspects in your attitude. Should any teacher so far lose control as to fly into a temper when these ruder symptoms of adolescence occur, he will lose all his power and authority as a teacher—as will the teacher who, when the children behave badly and make a great noise gets terribly angry and then says: 'If you don't stop that noise at once I shall throw the inkpots at your heads!' The children will no longer have any respect for him after that.

As for the girls, who bring the inner bashfulness to expression in a different way, you will need to respond with a certain delicacy and grace to even the more coquettish bad behaviour and then, figuratively speaking, turn away. So we should both respond with delicacy and grace to these things but give no sign that we take an interest. Leave the girl to it. Leave girls with a testy attitude to it.

With the boy, we should respond rather more explicitly to his behaviour, yet all the time making it plain that we do not take it very seriously; perhaps we can even laugh at it a little, but tactfully, so as not to upset him greatly.

The point is to acquire a certain intuitive feeling for how to treat children of this age; for every child differs from every other. The symptoms that occur arise from a metamorphosis of the bashfulness that permeates the child's whole being; and we will prepare him in the right way for his early twenties—and that is our task—if we keep always in mind that the subjective together with the astral body is now undergoing its independent development. And just as the human being's physical body needs strong, well-shaped bones if it is not to stumble about, so at this age the astral body with the ego enclosed within it needs ideals if it is to develop properly. I mean this in all earnestness. Ideals, will-like concepts, will-like ideals must now be introduced like a firm scaffolding into the astral body.

This need for ideals shows itself particularly in boys and it is up to us to discover this and approach it in the right way: each one must chose his hero whom he follows to the heights of Olympus. And it is of great importance to present boys with ideals as a reality, a figurative personality, or perhaps some mythical figure, or even an imaginary one that the boy constructs with our help out of his own imagination. And then, when we go for excursions with the children, we can converse with each one according to his individual character: how do you imagine you would set about undertaking this task, or that task? We talk to them of the future and of their aims and purposes in life. By so doing, we give a kind of firmness and strength to the astral body; and that is what is needed at this age.

The same has to be done also for the girl. But here we will best achieve our purpose when we remember that, as the boy inclines more to the earthly, so the girl to the cosmos. Girls are inclined more towards the cosmos, and when we want to lead the girl to find her ideal we should accordingly relate to her more the deeds of the heroes, we should tell what they did and what happened to them. For the girl, it will be facts and experiences; for the boy it will be the heroic figure in its completeness. So, you see, here again we have to take into account the differences between boys and girls.

2.4 Transformation of the human organism at the age of puberty

Just as the period of life at about the seventh year is significant in earthly existence on account of all the facts which I have described, so similarly there is a point in the earthly life of the human being which, on account of the symptoms which then arise in life, is no less significant. The actual points of time indicated are, of course, approximate, occurring in the case of some human beings earlier, in others later. The indication of seven-yearly periods is approximate. But round about the fourteenth or fifteenth year there is once more a time of extraordinary importance in earthly existence. This is the period when puberty is reached. But puberty, the emergence of the sexual life, is only the most external symptom of a complete transformation that has taken place in the human being between the seventh and fourteenth year. Just as we must seek in the growth-forces of the teeth—in the human head—for the physical origin of thought that frees itself about the seventh year of life and becomes a function of soul, so we must look for the activity of the second soul force, namely feeling, in other parts of the human organism.

Feeling releases itself much later than thinking from the

bodily nature, from the physical constitution of the human being. And between the seventh and fourteenth year the child's feeling life is still inwardly bound up with its physical organization. Thinking is already free; feeling is still inwardly bound up with the body. All the feelings of joy, of sorrow and of pain that express themselves in the child still have a strong physical correlation with the secretions of the organs, the acceleration or retardation, speed or slackening of the breathing system. If our perception is keen enough, we can observe in these very phenomena the great transformation that is taking place in the life of feeling, when the outer symptoms of the change make their appearance. Just as the appearance of the second teeth denotes a certain climax in growth, so the close of the subsequent life period—when feeling is gradually released from its connection with the body and becomes a soul function—is expressed in speech. This may be observed most clearly in boys. The voice changes; the larynx reveals the change. Just as the head reveals the change which lifts thinking out of the physical organism, the breathing system—the seat of the organic rhythmic activity—expresses the emancipation of feeling. Feeling detaches itself from the bodily constitution and becomes an independent function of soul. We know how this expresses itself in boys. The larynx changes and the voice gets deeper. In girls different phenomena appear in bodily growth and development, but this is only the external aspect.

Anyone who has reached the first stage of exact clairvoyance already referred to, the stage of imaginative perception, knows—for he perceives it—that the male physical body transforms the larynx at about the fourteenth year of life. The same thing happens in the female to the etheric body, or body of formative forces. The change withdraws to the etheric body, and the etheric body of the female takes on—as etheric body—a form exactly resembling the physical body of the male. Again, the etheric body of the male at the fourteenth year takes on a form resembling the physical body of the female. However extraordinary it may appear to a mode of knowledge that clings to the physical, it is nevertheless the case that from this all-important period of life onwards, the man bears within him etherically the woman, and the woman etherically the man. This is expressed differently in the corresponding symptoms in the male and female.

Now if one reaches the second stage of exact clairvoyance (it is described in greater detail in my books), if, beyond Imagination, one attains Inspiration—the actual perception of the independent spiritual element that is no longer bound up with the physical body of the human being—then one becomes aware how in actual fact in this important period round about the fourteenth and fifteenth years a third human component develops into a state of independence. In my books I have called this third being the astral body, according to an older tradition. This astral body is more essentially of the nature of soul than the etheric body; indeed the astral body is already of the soul and spirit. It is the third component of the human being and constitutes the second supersensory part of his being.

Up to the fourteenth or fifteenth year this astral body works through the physical organism and, at the fourteenth or fifteenth year, becomes independent. Thus teachers are faced with a very important task, namely to help the development to independence of this being of soul and spirit which lies hidden in the depths of the organism up to the seventh or eighth year and then gradually—for the process is successive—frees itself. It is this gradual process of detachment that we must assist if we are teaching the child between the ages of seven and 14. And then, if we have acquired the kind of knowledge of which I have spoken, we notice how the child's speech becomes quite different. The crude science of today—if I may call it so—concerns itself merely with the crude soul-qualities of the human being and refers to the other phenomena as secondary sexual characteristics. To spiritual observation, however, the secondary phenomena are primary, and vice versa.

2.5 Spiritual aspects of the women's question

This is an important point. Men have played a greater part because materialism is oriented towards external culture. This external culture is a man's culture because it was meant to be a material culture. But we must also be aware that in the development of world history one cultural epoch gives way to another, and that this one-sided masculine culture must find its completion through that which lives in every man. That was sensed precisely in the age of this masculine culture. That is why, when the mystics spoke from the innermost depths of their souls, they defined this soul as something feminine. Hence you find everywhere that the soul receptive to the world is compared with a woman; and it provides the basis for Goethe's words in the 'Chorus mysticus':

> Everything transient
> Is but a parable;
> All that's inadequate
> Here finds fulfilment;
> The indescribable
> Here it is done;

> The eternal feminine
> Bears us aloft.

It is nonsense to analyse this saying in a trivial way. It is interpreted rightly in the sense of Goethe and true mysticism when one says: anyone who knew something of noble spiritual culture also pointed to the feminine character of the soul; and precisely from this masculine culture did the words 'The eternal feminine bears us aloft' emerge. Thus the greater world, the cosmos, was pictured as a man and the soul, which was fertilized by the wisdom of the cosmos, as the feminine.

And what then is this peculiar way of thinking which has developed in men over the centuries, namely logic? If we wish to look into the depths of its nature, then we must see something feminine, the imagination, which must be fertilized by the masculine.

Thus, when we consider that which grows over and beyond the differences of gender, we see the higher nature of the human being—that which the 'I' creates out of the lower bodies. Man and woman must look on their physical body as an instrument which enables them, in one direction or another, to be active as a totality in the physical world. The more human beings are aware of the spiritual within them, the more does the body become an instrument, and the more do they learn to understand people by looking into the depths of the soul.

This will not give you a solution to the women's question, but it will give you a perspective. You cannot solve the women's question with trends and ideals! In reality you can only solve it by creating that concept, that disposition of soul which enables men and women to understand each other out of the totality of human nature. As long as people are preoccupied with matter, a truly fruitful discussion on the women's question will not be possible.

For this reason it should not surprise us that in an age that has given birth to a masculine culture the spiritual culture which began in the theosophical movement had to be born from a woman.[23] Thus the theosophical or spiritual-scientific movement will prove itself to be eminently practical. It will lead humanity to overcome gender in itself and to rise to the level where Spirit Man or Atman stands, which is beyond gender, beyond the personal—to rise to the purely human. Theosophy does not speak of the genesis and development of the human being in general but of general humanity, so that it is gradually recognized. Thus there will gradually awake in woman a consciousness similar to that which during this masculine culture has awoken in men. Just as Goethe, speaking from the depths of soul, once said, 'The eternal feminine bears us aloft,' so others too who as women feel in themselves the other side of the human being, and who in a truly practical sense understand it in terms of spiritual science, will speak of the eternal masculine in the feminine nature.

Then there will be a true understanding of and a true solution of soul for the women's question.

For external nature is the physiognomy of the soul life. We have nothing in our external culture other than what human beings have created, what human beings have translated from impulses into machines, into industry, into the legal system. In their development, external institutions reflect the development of the soul. An age, however, which clung to the outer physiognomy, was able to erect barriers between men and women. An age that is no longer entrenched in what is material, what is external, but which will receive knowledge of the inner nature of the human being which transcends sex, will, without wishing to crawl into bleakness or asceticism or to deny sexuality, enable and beautify the sexual and live in that element which transcends it. And people will then have an understanding for what will bring the true solution to the woman's question, because it will present at the same time the true solution to the eternal question of humanity. One will then no longer say, 'The eternal feminine bears us aloft,' or, 'The eternal masculine bears us aloft,' but, with deep understanding, with deep spiritual understanding one will say: 'The eternal human bears us aloft.'

2.6 *The equality of women and the unique individuality*

It is impossible to understand a human being fully if one's judgement of him is based on generic concepts. The tendency to do so is most persistent in regard to the sexes. Man sees in woman, and woman in man, nearly always too much of the general character of the other sex and too little of what is individual. In practical life this does less harm to men than to women. The social position of women is often so worthless because in many respects it is determined not by the individual qualities of the particular woman herself, as it should be, but by what is generally considered to be woman's natural tasks and needs. A man's activity in life is more directed towards his particular abilities and inclinations, whereas a woman's is largely determined by the fact that she is a woman. She is supposed to be a slave to her gender, to womanhood as such. As long as men debate whether a woman is suited to this or that profession 'according to her natural disposition', no progress will be made in the so-called women's question. What a woman, according to her nature, is capable of must be left to the woman to decide for herself. If it is true that women are fit only for the callings that are theirs at present, then they will hardly have it in them to attain any other. But women must be allowed to decide for themselves what is in accordance with their nature. To those who fear a social upheaval, should women be accepted as individuals rather than as members of their sex, it must be said that a social structure in which the status of one half of humanity is beneath the dignity of a human being is itself in great need of improvement.[24]

Those who judge human beings according to generic characteristics come to a halt at the borderline beyond which people begin to be individuals whose activity is based on their own free self-determination. What lies short of this borderline can naturally become the subject of scientific study. Racial, tribal, national and sexual characteristics are subjects of special sciences. Only people who wanted to live solely as examples of the genus could possibly fit the general picture that emerges from these scientific studies. None of these sciences come near to what is unique in the individual. Generic laws cease to be applicable to the individual once we are dealing with that aspect of his being where freedom begins (in thinking and acting). The conceptual content which a human being must connect with percepts by means of thinking in order to take hold of the full reality of things cannot be settled once and for all and bestowed ready-made on human beings. Each individual must attain his concepts through his own intuition. How the individual has to think cannot be deduced from any generic concept. That depends entirely on the individual himself. Nor are general human traits any indication of what concrete goals a person may set himself. If one is to understand another human being as an individual, one must penetrate to his essential nature and not stop short at typical characteristics. In this sense every human being sets us a problem. All knowledge concerned with theoretical and generic concepts is merely a preparation for the insight we gain when a human individuality shares with us his way of looking at the world, and that other insight we gain from knowing his intentions and wishes. Whenever we sense that we are dealing with an element in a person which is free from stereotypical thinking and generic desires, we must refrain from calling to our aid any concepts applicable to our own spirit if we are to understand him. Cognition consists in connecting the concept with the percept by means of thinking. In the case of all other objects the observer must attain the concepts through his intuition, but when it is a question of understanding a free individuality we must take over into our own spirit the concepts by which he defines himself, in their purity (without mingling them with any conceptual content of our own). People who immediately mix their own concepts into every judgement of others can never attain understanding of an individuality. Just as the free individuality frees himself from generic characteristics, so must the cognition by which we are to understand him free itself from the way we understand what is generic.

Only to the extent that a human being has freed himself from everything generic, in the way described, can he be said to be a free spirit within the human community. No human being is all genus, none is all individuality. But every person gradually liberates a greater or lesser part of his nature from the generic characteristics of animal life and from the domination of the decrees of human authorities.

3. Sex and its Attendant Problems

3.1

In this section we see Rudolf Steiner speaking as freely as he was able to for the time. Starting again with adolescence, he warns that if children reach puberty without an education based on spiritual insights, the changing forces of their astral bodies will lead to a thirst for power and excessive eroticism, plus too much brooding on themselves—all symptoms to be found today. His comments on the 'knowingness' of schoolgirls in 1922 shows that young people at that time were already not little innocents. Looking back then at the younger child, we learn something of child development and the mistaken ideas about young children's sexuality. In a wholesome way he alludes to the fact of their interest in their genitals being something that is not sexual in origin and parents should not treat it as something improper.

3.1.1 Education in adolescence

You see, it is really essential that in this respect exceptionally clear educational concepts should once more hold sway. One cannot say that they are at all prevalent today. Precisely when this age group is being considered, one can observe how people dwell on purely secondary issues. It has even reached the point where certain instinctive psychological processes occurring in children at puberty are being looked at, also in educational circles, in the light of a completely wrong analysis of the psychology involved.

In general, the following holds true. Once children reach puberty, it is necessary to awaken in them an unusually high measure of interest in their environment. Through the way they are instructed and educated they must see the world outside them with its processes, how it conforms to certain laws, how cause and effect, purpose and objective are at work within it.

This is so, of course, not just where a consideration of people's lives is concerned, but quite generally—even for such things as a piece of music. All these things should be presented to youngsters in such a way as to produce a constant echoing within them, so that questions arise about nature, about the cosmos and the world, about human nature in general, about historical issues and so on. Questions should arise within the young person regarding the enigmas of the world and its phenomena. For within the soul there are present at this age forces made available by the freeing of the astral body whose task it is to come to grips with such enigmas. If questions of this sort about the world and its phenomena do not arise within the young human being, these forces become transformed into something else. If one has not succeeded in arousing the most intense interest in the riddles of the world when the forces become available, they are then transformed into what is generally to be observed in the young people of today. They undergo transformation into something instinctive in two directions: firstly into a lust for power, and secondly into eroticism. The unfortunate thing is that it is assumed even in educational thinking that this lust for power and this eroticism are natural features of the human make-up from puberty onwards, rather than subordinate phenomena produced by the metamorphosis of things which, until the twentieth or twenty-first year, should be going in quite a different direction.

Essentially, if in the educational process the correct lines are being followed, it is quite unnecessary to speak to young people between the ages of 14 or 15 and 20 about the lust for power and about eroticism. These are things which take their course below the surface of conscious life. If they have to be spoken of at this age, that in itself is already something unhealthy. Our whole theory and practice of education suffer from constant focusing on this matter as something pre-eminent. The sole reason for the pre-eminence given to this question is that, in an age when materialism is the all-embracing world-view, people today have more and more lost the ability to arouse a genuine interest in the world—the world in the widest sense of the word. Our academic disciplines, in which, of course, today's teachers have also been educated, actually contain in essence nothing at all about the world. They offer physical laws, mathematical relationships, descriptions of what goes on within the cell and all manner of views about historical process that are open to debate. These things put together are quite incapable of inspiring interest in young people precisely between 15 and 20 years of age. Anyone sufficiently unprejudiced to make the proper observations in this area is bound to realize that such stuff is simply incapable of satisfying the deepest interests of those people in the age group we are discussing. Through the lack of sufficient interest in the world around them, they are thrown back upon themselves and thereby begin to brood over all manner of things.

By and large, one is obliged to say that the most unhealthy aspects of present-day civilization come about essentially because people are far too preoccupied with themselves; they spend a large part of their leisure time being concerned with their own well-being and whatever brings them personal comfort, rather than engaging themselves with the world

around. Of course, when the need is there, such personal
concerns may be perfectly legitimate. Indeed, if one is ill one
must attend to such things. However it is not only confined
to when they are ill that people are wrapped up in themselves;
it also happens when they are comparatively healthy.
Furthermore, the least favourable period to be preoccupied
with oneself is between the ages of 14 or 15 and 21. The
capacity for independent judgement, which blossoms at this
age, needs to be directed towards considering how the many
different aspects of the world interrelate. The world should
increasingly become so interesting for the young people that
it never occurs to them to divert their attention sufficiently
from it so as to be constantly preoccupied with themselves.
For as everyone knows, as far as the subjective sensation is
concerned pain increases the more one thinks about it. The
injury, considered objectively, does not; but when one is
forever thinking about it, the pain does. In some respects, the
best way of overcoming pain is if one can bring oneself not to
think about it. Now, what develops in the young person,
precisely at this time, is not wholly dissimilar to pain. The
process of learning to accommodate oneself to the effects of
the astral body as it establishes its independent activity within
the physical body really does produce a continual experience
of mild pain, the awareness of which immediately prompts
one to become preoccupied with oneself, unless one's
attention is sufficiently diverted towards what lies outside
oneself.

We cannot remind ourselves often enough that the
education of young people between 14 or 15 and 18 must be
founded in the most careful way possible on the fundamental, moral relationship between the teacher and the
pupil. 'Moral' in this respect is to be taken in its widest

possible sense. This means, for instance, that the teacher calls forth in his soul the deepest feelings of responsibility regarding his task.

In what I have put before you lies the possibility even in girls' schools of easily reducing the preoccupation with sex about which people today make such a great stir. Where alarmingly rampant eroticism is prevalent among youngsters of this age, it is the teachers who are at fault through their failure to be stimulating and to arouse interest in the world. If children have no interest in the world, what do you expect them to think about? If they are bored by the tedious way in which mathematics, history and so on are being taught, of course their thoughts will turn to what is going on within their bodies, in heart, stomach, lungs. Only by diverting interest towards the outside world will one ever prevent this happening, and such a great deal depends on our doing just that.

Actually, the prevalence of eroticism and especially the excessive concern with sexual matters in youngsters of this age, if they are still at school, can always be blamed on the school to some extent. For, you see, this unhealthy concern with sex, which is now so widespread even to outer observation, is basically only present in the cities and, what is more, among city people who have then become teachers and doctors.[25] It was only when city life came to completely dominate our civilization that such things came to—I can hardly call it flowering—to such a frightful state of degeneracy.

In relation to what we have been saying, the criminal psychologist and excellent medical doctor Moritz Benedikt was right when some ten years ago he had this to say regarding all the talk about perversion among young people,

homosexuality and generally all those things which are talked
about and dwelt on as if they need to be observed again and
again: 'The average girl at a boarding school today knows
more about these things than we young doctors did 30 years
ago.'[25a]

3.1.2 *The young child as an asexual being*

Let us consider the first significant phase of life, the phase up
to the change of teeth at approximately the seventh year. As
you know, this marks the end of the first significant stage of
human life. It is a very important time, a time marked also by
the appearance of a paradox that it is very important to
understand. For during the period leading to the change of
teeth at around the seventh year, those who observe a human
being physically are observing falsely. I have frequently
alluded to this from other points of view. To put it briefly,
people look upon a human being during the first seven years
as if it already were male or female. From a higher point of
view this is entirely false. But the materialism of today does
hold this view. That is why the materialists of today look
upon manifestations during the first seven years as if they
were already manifestations of sexuality, which is not at all
the case. Matters will be in a much healthier state when it is
understood that a child is an asexual being during its first
seven years, and not a sexual being at all. To use a trivial
expression, it only looks as though a child were already male
or female during the first seven years. This is because there is
no physical distinction between what one calls masculine or
feminine during the first seven years and what one calls
masculine and feminine later. For materialism, the physical
is all that there is, so what comes later seems to be a con-

tinuation of what was already there. But that is not the case at all. And I now ask you to really experience what I am saying, to take it into yourselves, so that it is not misunderstood and immediately mixed up with value judgements. What I say is meant objectively, so please do not fall into the pattern so often found in other areas today, whereby one judges on the basis of previously held values instead of judging objectively.

During the first seven years, what appears to be masculine is not masculine as such—and here I ask you to keep in mind what I have said about Uranus and Gaia;[26] it has the external form that it has in order that the heavenly forces working from the head can continue to influence the individual being and the human form in accordance with what is heavenly and lies outside earth. That is why it appears masculine. But it is not male; it is formed by Uranus in accordance with what lies outside earth! I said the head is the part of the human being where the heavenly takes precedence, the earthly takes precedence in the rest of the body. But the earthly radiates into the heavenly, just as the heavenly radiates into the earthly. Mutual relationships connect them; it is only a question of which one predominates. I would like to describe matters by saying that, with one kind of human being, the heavenly aspect is the preponderant influence on the body, including the parts other than the head, with the result that one says he is male. But this still has nothing to do with sexuality, but only with the fact that this particular organization is more Uranian, whereas in the case of other individuals their organization is more terrestrial, Gaian. During the first seven years, the human being is not a sexual being; that is maya. The bodies differ in that some show more how the heavenly side is at work and others show more from the earthly side. In anticipation of value judgements that might insinuate themselves into our discussions, I began by saying that from a universal point of view the earthly sphere has as much value as the heavenly. I did not want anyone to harbour the belief that we were devaluing the feminine, in the style of Weininger,[27] by taking some elevated, mystical standpoint that makes it out to be merely earthly or merely Gaian. Each is the pole of the other, and this has nothing to do with sexuality.

What, then, is going on in the human being, in the human organization, during the first seven years? You must take what I am going to describe as the predominant circumstances; the opposite is also there, but what I am characterizing is the predominant situation. For you see, during the first seven years the head is constantly being worked on by forces that stream to it from the rest of the organism. There are also forces that flow from the head to the rest of the organism, of course, but during this period these are relatively weak in comparison to the forces that stream from the body to the head. If the head grows and continues to develop during the first seven years, this is due to the fact that the body is actually sending its forces into the head; during the first seven years, the body imprints itself into the head and the head adapts to the bodily organization. With regard to human development, the essential thing during the first seven years is that the head becomes adapted to the bodily organization. This welling-up of the rest of the organization into the head is what is behind the distinctive facial metamorphoses that someone with a finely developed sense for it can observe during the first seven years. Just watch the development of a child's face, and observe how it changes at the time of the change of teeth, when the whole body is more or less poured into the facial expression.

Up to the change of teeth

Then comes the period that leads to sexual maturity—
roughly from the seventh to the fourteenth year. And now
exactly the opposite happens: the forces of the head flow
uninterruptedly down into the organism, into the body; now
the body adapts to the head. The resultant total revolution in
the organism is very interesting to watch. The welling-up of
the forces of the body into the head during the first seven
years concludes with the change of teeth. Then there is a
reversal in the flow of forces, which begin to stream downward. It is these downward-streaming forces that turn a
human being into a sexual being. Now, for the first time, the
human being becomes a sexual being. To begin with, what
turns the organs that are simply heavenly or earthly into
sexual organs comes from the head; and that is spirit. The
physical organs are not even intended for sexuality. That is
exactly the way to put it—they are only adapted to sexuality
later on. And the judgement of those who maintain that they
are originally adapted to sexuality is superficial. On the
contrary, the organs are adapted to the heavenly sphere in
one case, to the earthly sphere in the other. They first acquire

a sexual character during the period between the seventh and fourteenth year when this is introduced into them from without by the forces that stream down from the head. That is when a human being begins to become a sexual being.

Up to adolescence

It is extraordinarily important to form a precise view of these things, for in practice one is constantly being confronted by people who come with their very small children, complaining about sexual improprieties. But such things are not possible before the seventh year because nothing sexual is yet present, nothing that has sexual significance. In such cases there would be no point in dealing with it medically but one should do so in a normal way by stopping calling things by false names and surrounding them with false concepts. One should recover that holy innocence with which the ancients viewed such matters. Given their atavistic knowledge of the spiritual world, it never would have occurred to them to begin applying sexual terms to those who were still children. I have already alluded to these things in other contexts.

Later on, it will be our task to look at other currents and forces important to human development. For the moment, it will be helpful to concentrate our attention on the first 14 years of human development. Only through such things will you begin to see how true it is to say that external life is a life of maya—is the great deception. For it really is a deception that a human being seems to arrive in the world as a male or a female. A human being first becomes a sexual being through what is acquired by the head from the earth during the first seven years there.

3.2

The next three extracts deal with the confusion of sex and passion with love, and the particular spiritual beings involved. Lucifer is that spirit which seeks to wrest human beings away from the earth and its mission, who inspires pride and egotism, passion and self-satisfaction—hence the somewhat veiled comment about men presumably being encouraged to visit prostitutes 'for their health and well-being', whereas in fact this is an exploitation because there is no love for the female partner. This is followed by a piece showing the part played by the other main adversary, Ahriman, who seeks to bind the human being to the earth, and the more sinister evil beings the Asuras, who will attack the human ego by urging people towards sensuality and sexual excess, encouraging the notion that we are only animals. Only with the power of the Christ working through human karma can their effects be over-come. Christ forces (in a universal sense) include the development of wonder, compassion and conscience, which will draw people towards Him.

3.2.1 The luciferic influence on love

We can form an idea about how Lucifer can get at human beings in this way by considering with our soul's eye a phenomenon in human life that we will speak about later in more detail: the phenomenon of love in the widest sense of the word, the foundation of a true moral life in the world order of humanity. Concerning love in its widest sense, the following has to be said: when love appears in the physical sense world and has its effect on human life, it is absolutely protected from every unjustified luciferic attack if the love is for another person and for that other person's own sake. When we encounter another human being or a being belonging to another kingdom of nature in the physical world, that being meets us with certain qualities. If we are freely receptive to these qualities, if we are capable of being moved by them, they then command our love and we cannot help loving that other being. We are moved by the other being to love it.

Where the cause of love lies not in the one who loves but in the object of their love, this form and kind of love in the sense world is absolutely proof against every luciferic influence. But now if you observe human life, you will soon see that there is another kind of love in which a person loves because he himself has certain qualities that feel satisfied, or charmed, or delighted, when he can love this or that other being. Here he loves for his own sake; he loves because his disposition is like this or that, and this particular disposition finds its satisfaction in loving someone else.

This love, which one can call egoistic love, must also exist. It really has to be present in humankind. Everything we can love in the spiritual world, all the spiritual facts, everything that love can cause to live in us as a longing for and an impulse upwards into the spiritual world, to comprehend the beings of the spiritual world, to perceive the spiritual world— all this springs naturally from a sentient love for that world. However, this love for the spiritual must, not may—must come about necessarily for our own sake. We are beings whose roots lie in the spiritual world. It is our duty to make ourselves as perfect as we can. For our own sake we must love the spiritual world in order to draw as many forces as possible out of it into our own being. In spiritual love a personal, individual element—we can call it egoistic—is fully justified, for it detaches the human being from the sense world, it leads him upwards into the spiritual world, it leads him on to fulfil the necessary duty of continually advancing further and further towards perfection.

Now Lucifer has the tendency to mix these two worlds with each other. In human love, whenever a person loves in the physical sense world for himself with a trace of egoism, it occurs because Lucifer wants to make physical love similar to spiritual love. He can then root it out of the physical sense world and lead it into his own special kingdom. This means that all love that can be called egoistic and is not there for the sake of the beloved but for the sake of the one who loves is exposed to Lucifer's impulses.

If we consider what has been said, we will see that in this modern materialistic culture there is every reason to point out these luciferic allurements in regard to love, for a great part of our present-day outlook and literature, especially that of medicine, is permeated by the luciferic conception of love. We would have to touch on a rather delicate subject if we were to treat this in greater detail. The luciferic element in love is actually cherished by a large section of our medical science; men are told again and again—for it is the male world which is especially pandered to in this—that they must cultivate a certain sphere of love as necessary for their health, that is, necessary for their own sake. A great deal of advice is given in this direction and certain experiences in love recommended that do not spring from a love for the other being but because they are presumed indispensable in the life of the male. Such arguments—even when they are clothed in the robes of science—are nothing but inspirations of the luciferic element in the world; a large portion of science is penetrated simply by luciferic points of view. Lucifer finds the best recruits for his kingdom among those who allow such advice to be given to them and who believe that it is imperative for the well-being of their person to cultivate certain forms of love life. It is absolutely necessary for us to know such things.

3.2.2 The attack on the human ego

Without karma, no progress would be possible. Karma turns out to be a blessing for us inasmuch as it obliges us to rectify every error, to re-achieve the steps that thrust us back.

Karma was the consequence of the deeds of Ahriman. And now let us go further. In our days we are moving towards the epoch when other beings will draw near to the human being—beings who in the future lying before us will intrude more and more deeply into human evolution. Just as the luciferic spirits intervened in the Lemurian and the ahrimanic spirits in the Atlantean epoch, so our epoch too will see the gradual intrusion of beings. Let us be clear about the nature of these beings.

We said about the beings who intervened during the

Lemurian epoch: they entrenched themselves in the astral body of the human being, drew his interests, impulses and desires down into the earthly sphere. Where—to speak more precisely—did these luciferic beings entrench themselves?

You can only understand this on the basis of the structure set out in my book *Theosophy*.[28] There it is shown that in the human being we must distinguish, first, his physical body, then his etheric or life body and his astral body—or, as I have called it in the book, the sentient body or soul-body.

These are the three components with which the human being was endowed before his earthly existence. The foundation of the physical body was laid on Old Saturn, the etheric body on the Old Sun, the soul or sentient body on the Old Moon. On the earth was added the sentient soul, which is actually a transformation, an unconscious elaboration of the sentient body. Lucifer anchored himself in the sentient soul; and there he remains. The intellectual soul came into being through the unconscious transformation of the etheric body, a more detailed description of which is contained in the book *The Education of the Child*.[29] It was in this second soul component, the intellectual soul, the transformed part of the etheric body, that Ahriman established his footing. From there he lures the human being to false judgements about material things, leads him to error, sin, lying—to everything that originates in the intellectual or mind soul. In every illusion that matter is the sole reality we must perceive the whispered promptings of Ahriman, of Mephistopheles. Thirdly, there is the consciousness soul, arising from an unconscious transformation of the physical body. You will remember how this transformation came about. Towards the end of the Atlantean epoch, the etheric body corresponding to the head came right into the physical head and gradually brought about self-consciousness in the physical body. Fundamentally speaking, the human being is still working at this unconscious transformation of the physical body, at the development of the consciousness soul. And in the age now approaching, those spiritual beings known as the Asuras will creep into the consciousness soul and thus into the human 'I', for the 'I' arises in the consciousness soul. The Asuras will generate evil with a far mightier force than was wielded by the satanic powers in the Atlantean epoch or by the luciferic spirits in the Lemurian epoch.

In the course of the earth period man will cast away all the evil brought to him by the luciferic spirits together with the blessing of freedom. The evil brought by the ahrimanic spirits can be shed in the course of the laws of karma. But the evil brought by the asuric powers cannot be expunged in this way. Whereas the good spirits instituted pain and suffering, illness and death in order that, despite the possibility of evil, the human being's evolution may still advance, whereas the good spirits made possible the working of karma to the end that the ahrimanic powers might be resisted and the evil made good, it will not be so easy to counter the asuric powers as earth existence takes its course. For these asuric spirits will prompt what has been seized hold of by them, namely the very core of the human being, the consciousness soul together with the 'I', to unite with the matter of the earth. Fragment after fragment will be torn out of the 'I' and, in the same measure in which the asuric spirits establish themselves in the consciousness soul, the human being must leave parts of his existence behind on the earth. What thus becomes the prey of the asuric powers will be irretrievably lost. Not that the whole of the human being need become their victim, but parts of his spirit will be torn away by the asuric powers. These asuric powers are heralded today by the prevailing tendency to live wholly in the material world and to be oblivious of the reality of spiritual beings and spiritual worlds. True, the asuric powers corrupt the human being today in a way that is more theoretical than actual. Today they deceive him by various means into thinking that his 'I' is a product of the physical world only; they lure him to a kind of theoretical materialism. But as time goes on—and the signs of this are the dissolute, sensuous excesses that are becoming increasingly prevalent on earth—they will blind the human being's vision of the spiritual beings and spiritual powers. The human being will know nothing nor desire to know anything of a spiritual world. More and more he will not only teach that the highest moral ideals of humanity are merely sublimations of animal impulses, that human thinking is but a transformation of a faculty also possessed by the animals, that the human being is akin to the animal in respect of his form and, moreover, in his whole being descends from the animal, but he will take this view in all seriousness and order his life in accordance with it.

The human being does not as yet entirely base his life on the principle that his true being descends from the animal. But this view of existence will inevitably arise, with the result that human beings will also live like animals, will sink into animal impulses, animal passions. And in many things that need not be further characterized here, many things that in the great cities come to expression in orgies of dissolute sensuality, we can already perceive the lurid, hellish glare of the spirits we call the Asuras.

Let us recap once more. We have said that suffering and pain, even death, were brought by the spirits who are intent upon the human being's progress. The words of the Bible are unambiguous: 'In sorrow thou shalt bring forth children.'

Death has come into the world. Death was decreed for the human being by the powers opposing the luciferic spirits. From whom did karma come, who made karma possible at all for the human being? To understand what is being said here, you must discard all earthly, pedantic notions of time. Earthly notions of time give rise to the belief that what has once happened here or there will have an effect only on what comes afterwards. But in the spiritual world it is the case that what comes to pass reveals itself in its effect beforehand; in its effect it is already there in advance. From where does the blessing of karma come? From where has there arisen in our earth evolution this blessing of karma? Karma comes in the whole of development from a power none other than Christ.

3.2.3 *Christ and the power of wonder, compassion and conscience*

But how does this Christ-spirit acquire his spiritual components? In the Mystery of Golgotha he descended into the sphere of earth as an impulse, as the soul of the earth.

It does not happen in the same way as in human beings, but the Christ-being too must form for himself something that can be called the components of His being. Christ will eventually have a kind of spiritualized physical body, a kind of etheric body and a kind of astral body. Of what will these bodies consist?

These are questions which for the time being can only be hinted at. When the Christ-being descended to the earth He had to provide Himself with something similar to the components of a human being: a physical body, an etheric body and an astral body. Gradually, in the course of the epochs, something that corresponds to an astral, an etheric and a physical body formed around the originally purely spiritual Christ-impulse which descended at the baptism by John. All these components are formed from forces which have to be developed by humanity on earth. What kind of forces are they?

The forces of external science cannot produce a body for Christ because they are concerned only with things that will have disappeared in the future, that will no longer exist. But there is something that precedes knowledge and is infinitely more valuable for the soul than knowledge itself. It is what the Greek philosophers regarded as the beginning of all philosophy: wonder or astonishment. Once we have the knowledge, the experience which is of value to the soul has really already passed. People in whom the great revelations and truths of the spiritual world can evoke wonder, nourish this feeling of wonder, and in the course of time this creates a force which has a power of attraction for the Christ-impulse, which attracts the Christ-spirit: the Christ-impulse unites with the individual human soul when the soul can feel wonder about the mysteries of the world. Christ draws his astral body in earthly evolution from all those feelings which have lived in single human souls as wonder.

The second quality that must be developed by human souls to attract the Christ-impulse is a power of compassion. Whenever the soul is moved to share in the suffering or joy of others, this is a force which attracts the Christ-impulse; Christ unites Himself with the human soul through com-passion and love. Compassion and love are the forces from which Christ forms his etheric body until the end of earthly evolution. With regard to compassion and love one could, to put it crudely, speak of a programme which spiritual science must carry out in the future. In this connection, materialism has evolved a pernicious science, such as has never previously existed on earth. The very worst offence committed today is to correlate love and sexuality. This is the worst possible expression of materialism, the most devilish symptom of our time. Sexuality and love have nothing whatever to do with each other. Sexuality is something quite different from and has no connection at all with pure, original love. Science has brought things to a shameful point by means of an extensive literature devoted to connecting these two things which are simply not connected.

A third force which flows into the human soul as if from a higher world, to which the human being submits, to which he attributes a higher significance than that of his own individual moral instincts, is conscience.

Christ is most intimately united with the human being's conscience. Christ draws his physical body from the impulses that spring from the conscience of individual human souls.

3.3

The causes of illness are complex and usually go back to previous incarnations—a fact which is unpalatable for many today. Rudolf Steiner often spoke of luciferic and ahrimanic influences and characterized their involvement with different illnesses. Here he mentions one which is the result of sexual excess. We do not usually associate sex with clairvoyance, but in the second extract Steiner gives us important guidance on how the sex force if misused during adolescence (it is unfortunately not explicit as to what exactly constitutes misuse) can result in distorted perceptions of previous earth lives. Not unconnected with this is the fact that with clair- voyant crossing into the spiritual world we also enter the realm of the dead, and the immediate astral realm, though 'higher' is also linked to lower human impulses on earth through our more animal instincts. We can see something of this with the state of drawing near to sleep—the dead can approach us when we are close to sleep—but it is also a state that for some people can give rise to sexual fantasies.

3.3.1 Pneumonia and sexual excess

Thus in the human individuality which goes through incarnations on the earth there is a luciferic influence and, as a result of this, the ahrimanic influence. These two powers are continually fighting in the human individuality, which has become their field of battle.

The human being in his ordinary consciousness is still exposed to the allurements of Lucifer which work from the passions and emotions of his astral body; also he is subject to the enticements of Ahriman, which come to him from outside in the way of error, deception, and so forth, in regard to the outer world. Therefore, as long as a person is incarnated on the earth with his mental images forming barriers, so that the influence of Lucifer and Ahriman cannot penetrate deeper but is hindered by these mental images or ideas, his acts will be guided by his moral or intellectual judgement. When a person between birth and death sins against morality in following Lucifer, or against logic or sound thinking in following Ahriman, that concerns only his ordinary conscious soul life. When, on the other hand, he passes through the portal of death, the life of ideas which is bound to the instrument of the brain ceases, and a different form of consciousness begins. Then all the things which in the life between birth and death are subject to a person's moral or rational judgement penetrate down into the foundation of the human being, into that which, after kamaloca,[30] organizes the next existence and imprints itself into the formative forces, which then construct a threefold human body. Errors resulting from devotion to Ahriman develop into forces of disease that affect the human being through his etheric body, whereas misdemeanours that are subject to one's moral judgement in life develop into causes of disease that tend to originate in the astral body.

From this we see how, in fact, our errors from the ahrimanic forces within us, including such conscious errors as lies and so on, develop into causes of disease if we do not merely consider the one incarnation but observe the effect of one incarnation on the next. We see also how the luciferic influences in the same way become the causes of disease, and we may in fact say that our errors do not go unpunished. We bear the stamp of our errors in our next incarnation. But we do this from a higher reason than that of our ordinary consciousness—from a consciousness which during the period between death and a new birth directs us to make ourselves so strong that we shall no longer be exposed to these temptations. Thus in our life disease even plays the part of a great teacher. If we study illnesses in this way we shall see unmistakably that an illness is a manifestation of either luciferic or ahrimanic influences. When these things are understood by those who will practise healing according to the principles of spiritual science their influence on the human organism will be infinitely more profound than it can be today.

We can examine certain forms of disease from this standpoint. Let us take pneumonia, for example; it is a karmic effect which follows when during his life in kamaloca the person in question looks back to a character which had within it the tendency towards sexual excess, and a desire to live a sensual life. Do not confuse what is now ascribed to a previous consciousness with what appears in the consciousness in the following incarnation. This is quite a different matter. Indeed, that which a person sees during his life in kamaloca will so transform itself that forces are imprinted in him by means of which he will overcome pneumonia. For it is exactly in the overcoming of this disease, in the self-healing which is then striven for, that the human individuality acts in opposition to the luciferic powers and wages a pitched battle against them. Therefore in overcoming pneumonia the opportunity is given to lay aside that which was a defect in the character in a previous incarnation. In this disease we see unmistakably our battle against the luciferic powers.

3.3.2 Clairvoyance and the lower instincts

Curiously enough, the capacity to see into one's own life or that of another in the spiritual world comes from the forces of the etheric body that have been saved over from the process of learning to walk. But seership shows that these forces, when they have really unfolded, are in a certain respect superior to the forces of clairvoyance developed with the object of looking back into earlier earth lives. Please take particular notice of this difference, for it throws light on many things.

There is no easier way of unfolding a dangerous form of clairvoyance than by the development of those forces which in the modern human being are there for the purpose of producing the organs of speech and which, if kept back, enable him to look into earlier incarnations; for these forces are connected most closely of all with the lower instincts and passions in the human being's nature. And by nothing is a human being brought so near to Lucifer and Ahriman as by the development of these forces which, at a certain level, enable him to look back into his own earlier earth lives or into those of others. They lead to illusions; but above all, if they are not rightly developed, they have the effect that under their influence the clairvoyant may deteriorate morally, rather than the reverse. So the very forces that make vision of earlier incarnations possible are the most dangerous of all. They should be unfolded only when at the same time the person pays full attention to the development of pure morality in his own being. Because morality in its purest form is essential if it is desired to unfold these forces, experienced teachers will not readily countenance any systematic development of the powers that enable a person to look into earlier incarnations.

Moreover this can be said: it is as common to find a certain lower kind of clairvoyance, which looks into other worlds and can give descriptions of spiritual regions, as it is rare to find evidence of the development of genuine, objective vision into earlier incarnations as the result of the exercise of the forces of speech alone. As a rule, therefore, recourse is had to yet other measures when it is desired to train the capacity to look back into earlier incarnations. And here we come to an interesting point, showing how necessary it is to pay attention to things of which otherwise little account is taken.

It will seldom happen that spiritual guidance brings a person to the point of being able, merely by the development of the forces of speech, to look back to earlier lives on earth. In the present age many individuals could be capable of this, but as a rule it is achieved by different means. One of these means will seem strange, although it is based on a profound truth.

Suppose someone lives intensely in his inner life. It would cost him excessive strain or possibly lead to overpowering temptations were he to succeed merely by developing the forces of speech to look back in the light of karma at his earlier incarnations. Hence the spiritual powers have recourse to different means. Apparently by chance, he meets someone who mentions a name or a particular epoch or people. This works on his soul from outside in such a way that the mental picture sets in motion the forces that help to promote clairvoyance. And then he becomes aware that this name or reference—although the speaker himself knew nothing about it—is a pointer, helping him to look into earlier lives on earth. In such a case there has been recourse to outer means. The human being in question hears the name of a person or of an epoch or of a people and is thus stimulated from outside to look back into previous incarnations. Such stimuli are sometimes exceedingly important for clairvoyant contemplation of the world. An experience seems to have been quite accidental but it provides a stimulus for powers of clairvoyance that would otherwise have remained rudimentary.

These are aphoristic indications on the subject of the penetration of the spiritual world into our earthly world. Actually, of course, the process is highly complicated.

Looking back into earlier earth lives is therefore connected with forces fraught with danger because they lead to deception, to delusion. On the other hand, hardly anyone who develops the forces of clairvoyance leading to insight into the life in the spirit preceding birth will be prone to misuse these forces. As a rule it will be souls of a certain purity, in whom there is a certain natural morality, who look back with reliable vision into the life in the spiritual world preceding the present life on earth. This is connected with the fact that the forces of clairvoyance used for looking into this particular period of existence are the forces of childhood, those that have been left over from the process of learning to walk. They are the most innocent of all the forces in the human being's nature.

I ask you to pay attention to this, for it is very significant. The most innocent forces are at the same time those which, when they are developed, enable a person to look into the life preceding birth. That, too, is why there is such enchantment in the sight of a tiny child, for in the aura playing around it are the forces which still send their radiance into the life before birth. In the aura of a child whose very countenance bears the stamp of innocence and otherworldliness, clairvoyant contemplation may perceive something that is truly more interesting than what comes to expression in the aura of many a grown-up person. The conflicts that were passed through in the spirit land before birth and determine the child's destiny make the aura round the child into something full of glory, full of wisdom. The wisdom manifesting in the aura of a child is often far greater than anything which at a later age he will be able to express in words. The physiognomy may still lack definition, but very much can be revealed to the clairvoyant when he is able to see what is playing around a child. And if the forces present in childhood are developed later on into clairvoyance, vision becomes possible of the actual conditions preceding birth by a considerable period.

To look into this world may not perhaps be gratifying to egoism, but to one who wishes to understand the whole setting of world existence this vista, too, is of absorbing interest. Investigation in the Akasha Chronicle[31] concerning certain outstanding figures in world history consists not only in trying to discover what kind of life they lived on the physical plane, but how as souls in the spiritual world between death and rebirth they made preparation for this life.

The forces which, if kept unsullied, shine into earlier incarnations are saved not so much in childhood but in the period of life when passions, moreover often in their worst form, unfold in the human being. These forces, which of course have other functions as well in human nature, develop much later than those of speech. They have to do with the emotions of sensual love and everything connected with them. There is a direct relationship between the forces leading to sensual love and those leading to speech—in the male this comes to expression in the breaking of the voice. It is at this age in life that many of these forces are saved. If they are kept pure they lead to the retrospective vision of earlier lives on earth. If they are not kept pure, if they come to be associated with sensual instincts in the human being, they may lead to the greatest occult abuses. The forces of clairvoyance which originate and are held back at this age in life are also those that are most easily subject to temptation. You will now be able to grasp the whole connection!

The seer who is happy to speak about the period stretching between death and rebirth—some of you will have noticed that in other circles this is seldom mentioned—such a seer has developed particularly the forces saved from very early childhood. But a clairvoyant who speaks a great deal—fallaciously for the most part—about the earlier incarnations of individuals must be distrusted. Some cases occur very frequently, for many people come out with utterances about earlier incarnations as if they were two-a-penny! A clairvoyant of this type must be distrusted because in this domain it is all too easy to evoke the forces most liable to temptation. The forces that can be saved for this purpose are saved at the time of life when sensual love is developing, and before the human being has taken his place in the social life. At times these forces give rise to a great deal of malpractice, especially to a definite occult malpractice, because they, more than any others, contribute to the promotion of delusion after delusion in the domain of the spiritual world.

Why are the assertions of clairvoyants who are exposed to these temptations so often false? It is because when the forces saved from this age of life are applied the lower instincts and urges immediately rise out of the human being like mist. And then Ahriman and the ahrimanic spirits approach and out of this rising mist create ghosts, spectres, which can be seen and taken to be earlier incarnations.

3.3.3 *The realm of the dead and the lower human impulses*

The other is what may be called direct interaction with beings of the spiritual world, and we will now speak of the interaction that is possible between those still living on earth and the so-called dead.

Such interaction is most certainly possible but it presents greater difficulties than the first form of knowledge, which is easy to attain. Actual interaction with an individual who has died is possible but difficult, because it demands scrupulous vigilance on the part of the one who seeks to establish it. Control and discipline are necessary for this kind of interaction with the spiritual world because it is connected with a very significant law. Impulses recognized as lower impulses in human beings on earth are, from the spiritual side, higher life. And it may therefore easily happen that when the human being has not achieved true control of himself he experiences the rising of lower impulses as the result of direct interaction with the dead. When we make contact with the spiritual world in the general sense, when we acquire knowledge about our own immortality as beings of soul and spirit, there can be no question of the entry of anything impure. But when it is a matter of contact with individuals who have died, the relationship of the individual dead person—strange as it seems—is always a relationship with the blood and nervous system. The dead person enters into those impulses which act in the blood and nervous system, and in this way lower impulses may be aroused. Naturally, there is only danger for those who have not purified their nature through discipline and control. This must be said, for it is the reason why in the Old Testament it is forbidden to have interaction with the dead. Such interaction is not sinful when it happens in the right way. The methods of modern spiritualism must, of course, be avoided. When the interaction is of a spiritual nature it is not sinful, but when it is not accompanied by pure thoughts it can easily lead to the stimulation of lower passions. It is not the dead who arouse these passions but the element in which the dead live. For consider this: what we feel here as animalistic in quality and nature is the basic element in which the dead live. The kingdom in which the dead live can easily change into its opposite when it enters into us; what is higher life there can become lower impulses when it is within us. It is very important to remember this, and it must be emphasized when we are speaking of inter-action between the living and the so-called dead, for it is an occult fact. But precisely when we speak about such inter-action, the spiritual world can be described as it really is, for such experiences reveal that the spiritual world is completely different from the physical world.

3.4

In the next two extracts the themes become more complex. Rudolf Steiner is making a connection between an ancient knowledge of star constellations and how in the past reproduction was guided by this. He touches on older beliefs of the Jews, Egyptians and Greeks and how they could perceive what lived spiritually in the air. We are all born into a specific family or bloodline, so these reproductive forces also relate to our nationality and here another abuse can arise. Sex instincts are linked to chauvinistic, nationalistic ones— a fact unknown to most people. As with the upsurge of sexual excesses in recent years we have seen a comparable rise in nationalism—usually of a negative kind. The antidote to chauvinism is brotherliness, and here we learn how the angelic beings are trying to lead humanity towards this state. Perhaps the recent growth of interest in angels is part of this. However, the passage includes a dire warning of what will happen if humanity has not grown more awake to the spiritual by the beginning of the third millennium—there will be an increase in sexual aberrations. We can conclude that the spiritual awakening is still insufficient.

3.4.1 Changes in consciousness and the sexual forces in connection with nationalism

These ancient peoples—and we could speak of others besides the Egyptians and the Greeks—these ancient peoples knew that the more inward-lying forces of human nature are connected with what comes to expression in celestial happenings, in star constellations. The decadence of the human being which is expressed in the modern attitude to the issue of sex, and that greatest decadence which is expressed in the most modern attitude to the issue of sex, of this nothing was yet known to those ancient peoples of the ages of which one must speak when one deals with these things. For them it was something very different when they had the feeling: it is the sexual essences which are suffused into the human being when the voice breaks and the thoughts break too at the same time, or when the other happens of which I have spoken. That the divine was then spreading through the human being—that was the conviction of the ancients. Hence what is only viewed in a corrupted sense today is found in all old religious rites: the sexual symbols, the so-called sexual symbols, point to this connection—we can call it the connection between the air with its air events and the human processes of knowledge which take place during the whole of human life between birth and death.

Through my eyes and through my ears—so said these people—I am connected with what the day brings. Through the deeper, more inwardly lying forces I am connected with something quite different, with the secrets of the air, which, however, are only perceived in imaginative experience. And this imaginative experience in its concrete form I have described for you with reference to these early times.

The Old Testament conception in these matters was different inasmuch as it put doctrine in the place of actual experience. The Egyptian in the age of Osiris, especially in the earlier period of the age of Osiris, said the following: 'The true human being only enters me with puberty, for I then assimilate what previously I saw in imaginations. The air transmits to me the true human being.' In the doctrine of the Old Testament this was transformed into the view that the Elohim or Yahweh have breathed into the human being the living breath, the air. There the essence was lifted out of the direct living experience and became doctrine, theory. This

was necessary, for only in this way could humankind be led—
and that is the meaning of the Old Testament—from that
living in union with the outer world, which still had an inner
connection between the microcosm, the human being, and
the macrocosm, the world, to its further evolution (of which I
will speak later). As this connection gradually vanished, it
was necessary to fall back on just such a doctrine as that of the
Old Testament.

But now there came the time of the death of Osiris—and
with that the time came too in which one thing became finer
and the other, as it were, coarser. How is that to be understood? Well, you can imagine it like this. When we go back
into the previous time of Osiris, the human being saw or felt
before puberty the light imaginations within the outer air [see
sketch]—if I speak about the one kind.

Thus he saw in his environment the light imaginations in
the air up to the time of puberty. Afterwards he had the

feeling that they had entered into him, and the changes occurred of which we have spoken. For the child, the air was everywhere filled with light phenomena; for the adult, the mature adult, the air was certainly still there but he knew that as child he had seen something else in it. He knew that the air was at the same time the bearer, the mother, of light. He knew that it was not true that when he looked out into the air there was nothing in it but what was revealed physically. Beings live in it which are perceived through Imagination.

For the Greeks, these beings belonged to the group around Zeus. Thus human beings knew that there were beings in the air. But all this—the fact that the human states of consciousness changed—all this is connected with the fact that even objective things became different in their finer state. Naturally for modern, clever people it is an outrage if one says such things. I know it is an outrage, but nevertheless it is true: the air has become different. Naturally it has not changed in a way that can be tested by chemical reagents; nevertheless the air has become different. The air has lost the strength to express the light imaginations; the air has—one could say—become coarser. It has actually become different on earth since that ancient time. The air has become coarser. Not only the air, however, but the human being himself has become coarser. That which formerly lived spiritually in the essences which permeated the larynx and the rest of the organism, that has also grown coarser. So that in fact if one speaks today of sexual essences one is referring to something that is different from what one would have referred to in ancient times. Everyone in those times knew: 'Daytime perception is connected with my personality; the other, which I experience from the air, experience with my whole life, that is connected with humankind as such, that goes beyond the individual person.' Hence they also sought to fathom the social mysteries under which human beings live together through the link which bound them with the macrocosm—they sought social wisdom through the star wisdom. What lived in the human being as social wisdom bound him in fact to the celestial. This came to expression in the most ordinary concepts. A human couple before the death of Osiris would never have felt anything else than that they had received a child from heaven. That was a living consciousness and corresponded also with the truth. And this living consciousness could develop because human beings knew that they received out of the air-filled space what they themselves experienced.

Of all this the coarse dregs, we might say, have been left. As in the air the coarse sediment has remained behind of that power of the air that revealed itself to the human being in imaginations in earlier ages, so in the human being himself the coarse dregs have been left behind. This had to come about since otherwise human beings could not have attained freedom and full ego consciousness. But it is the dregs that have remained. In this way, however, all that the ancients meant by the divine, which as you can now readily realize they connected in a roundabout way with the sexual essences, all this has been coarsened not only in idea but also in reality. But it is there nevertheless; naturally not only in the one way, but in the other way too. The reproduction of humankind was in those ancient times thought to be directly connected with humankind's bond between the microcosm and the macrocosm, as you have seen. Indeed, the whole social life of human beings on earth was in fact also thought to be connected with the bond between the microcosm and the macrocosm. Numa Pompilius[32] went to the nymph

Egeria to receive information from her as to how he should arrange social conditions in the Roman Empire. What this means, however, is that he had let the star wisdom be imparted to him, had let the star wisdom tell him how social conditions should be organized.

That which human beings reproduce on earth, and which is connected with successive generations, was to be placed in the service of what the stars have to say. Just as the individual human being directed his life with his ordinary perception and thinking according to the rising and setting of the sun, so the interconnections of humankind which later became 'states' were to be placed under the star constellations as an expressions of the cosmic relationships.

In our [German] language—and languages often reflect ancient memories—we still have a memory of this connection in the fact that masculine and feminine is described by the word *Geschlecht* (gender) and successive generations are also described as *Geschlechter* (lineage). It is one and the same word, *Geschlecht*—meaning interconnected family, blood relationship, as well as the state of masculine and feminine. And so is it too in other languages, and it all points to how the human being sought to find a recognizable connection with the macrocosm for what lay in his nature, in the deeper strata of his being.

These things have become coarsened in the direction we have discussed. Among other things that have remained behind is the attachment in longing and feeling to nationality, the clinging to the national, the chauvinistic impulse for the national; that is the lingering relic of what in older times could be thought of in quite a different context. But only when one looks into such things does one know the truth contained in them. What is expressed by nationalistic longing? When human beings develop such national feeling to excess, what does such sentiment with regard to the nation contain? Exactly the same as lives in the sexual, it is in the sexual in one way, in national sentiment in another. It is the sexual human being that lives his life through these two different poles. To be chauvinistic is nothing other really than developing a sort of group sexuality. One could say that there is greater national chauvinism where what has been left behind by the sexual essences takes hold of human beings to a greater extent; for it is the very force living in reproduction that comes to manifestation too in national sentiment. Hence the battle cry for so-called 'freedom of peoples or of nations' is really only to be understood in its more intimate connections if one refers—in a most respectable sense of course—to a 'call for the re-establishment of the national in the light of the sexual problem'. It is necessary to realize, as one of the secrets of the impulse of our time, the fact that the sexual problem is proclaimed in quite a special form across the earth today, without people having any idea of how out of their subconscious the sexual clothes itself in the words: 'Freedom of the peoples'. And sexual impulses are present in the catastrophic events of today far more than people imagine! For the impulses for what is happening today lie, in fact, very, very deep.

Such truths must no longer be kept under lock and key in our present age. Certain brotherhoods have been able to keep them under lock and key because in the strictest sense of the word they have excluded women. Although working together with women can still lead to all sorts of bad things, as has been shown in various ways,[33] yet the time has come in which correct views, general views, on these matters must spread among humanity. After all, ideas are spread abroad which are impure, foolish, empty, inasmuch as from certain directions, without knowledge of the more intimate connections, all sorts of things are treated today as sexual problems. But you see how what here is pure, genuine, honourable truth comes in contact, on the one hand, with what can be the most impure, filthiest way of thinking, as can be seen occasionally in the excesses of psychoanalysis or similar things. You will always find, however, that what on the one hand, rightly understood, is profound truth does not need to be altered very much in words, but only to be permeated with a filthy attitude, and it is simply a filthy, stupid, objectionable view.

A former age could speak of 'nations' when nations were pictured in such a way that one nation had its guardian spirit in Orion, another in another star, and people knew that these things were regulated by the constellations. One appealed, as it were, to the order of the heavens. Today where there is no longer such a heavenly order, the appeal is merely to the national, the chauvinistic appeal is merely to the national—in other words, the assertion of a luciferic impulse which in the most eminent way is a backward psycho-sexual one.

3.4.2 The work of the angels in our astral body

Where are we to look for this work of the angels? Today we still find it in human sleep states, including states of waking sleep. I have often said that even when they are awake people actually sleep through the most important concerns in life. And I can assure you, though you may not be pleased to hear it, that anyone who goes through life with a wide-awake mind will find numbers and numbers of people who are really asleep. They let events happen without taking the slightest interest in them, without troubling their heads over them or connecting with them in any way. Great world events often pass people by just as something happening in the city passes by someone who is asleep; yet those people are ostensibly awake. When people are thus sleeping through some momentous event it can be seen that the angels are doing their important work in their astral bodies—quite independently of what these people do or do not want to know.

Such things often happen in a way which must necessarily seem highly enigmatic and distinctly odd. We may think some people completely unworthy of entering into any connection with the world of the spirit. But the truth may well be that in this incarnation the person is an absolute dormouse who sleeps through everything that goes on around him. And in his astral body a spirit from the community of angels is working on the future of mankind. Observation of this astral body shows that it is being used in spite of those conditions.

What really matters, however, is that human beings grow conscious of these things. The consciousness soul must rise to the level where it is able to recognize what can only be discovered in this particular way.

You will now have sufficient background to understand me when I say that this age of the consciousness soul is moving towards a specific event. Because it involves the consciousness soul you will understand that the effect this event has on human evolution will depend on human beings themselves. This may be a century earlier or a century later, but it is bound to be part of the evolutionary process. It can be characterized by saying that purely out of the consciousness soul, purely out of conscious thinking, human beings must reach the point of actually perceiving what the angels are doing to prepare the future of humanity. The things we learn through the science of the spirit must become practical wisdom in the life of humanity—so practical that people will be convinced it is part of their own wisdom to recognize the aims of the angels as I have described them.

The progress of the human race towards freedom has already reached a point where it will depend on human beings themselves whether they are going to sleep through this event or face it in wide-awake consciousness. To meet it in full consciousness would mean this: we can study the science of the spirit. Indeed nothing else is really necessary. It also helps to meditate and use the guidance given in *Knowledge of the Higher Worlds.*[34] But the essential step has already been taken if the science of the spirit has been studied and really consciously understood. Today it can be studied without developing clairvoyant faculties.

Everyone can do so who does not bar his own way with his prejudices. And if people study the science of the spirit more and more thoroughly, assimilating its concepts and ideas, their conscious mind will become so alert that they will be fully aware of events and no longer sleep through them.

We can characterize these events in greater detail. Essentially knowing what the angel is doing is only a preparation. The important point is that three things will happen at a particular point in time. As I said, depending on how people respond, the time may be earlier or later or at worst they may not happen at all. But the intention is that humanity shall be shown three things by the angelic world.

Firstly, it will be shown that their own genuine interest will enable people to understand the deeper side of human nature. A time will come—and it must not pass unnoticed—when human beings will receive an impulse from the world of the spirit through the angel. This will kindle a far deeper interest in every human individual than we are inclined to have today. Enhanced interest in other human beings will not be of the subjective kind we like to develop at our leisure, but there will be a sudden impetus and a secret will be instilled into us from the realm of the spirit—the secret of what the other person really is. This is something quite real and specific, not any kind of theoretical consideration. People will learn something and this will kindle their interest in every human being. This is the one event, and it will particularly affect the social sphere.

The second event will be that the angel irrefutably shows the human being that apart from all else the Christ-impulse means complete religious freedom for humanity and that the only true Christianity is one that makes absolute religious freedom possible.

The third event will be that we gain irrefutable insight into the spiritual nature of the world.

As I have said, the three events should take place in such a way that the consciousness soul in us participates in it. This is something that will happen in human evolution, with the angels now working to this end through the images they create in the human astral body.

Let it be emphasized, however, that this impending triple event is subject to the human being's free will. Many things that should lead to conscious awareness of the event may be and indeed are being left undone.

As you know, other spirits involved in world evolution have an interest in deflecting humankind from its proper course. These are the ahrimanic and luciferic spirits. The events I have just described are part of the divine evolution of the human being. If people were to follow the dictates of their own true nature they could not really fail to perceive what the angels are doing in their astral body. But luciferic spirits seek to divert human beings concerning insight into the work of the angels. They do this by curbing free will. They try to cloud our understanding of the exercise of our free will. True, they desire to make us good—from the point of view from which I am now speaking Lucifer desires goodness, spirituality, for humankind—but he wants to make us into automatons, with no free will. Human beings are to be made clairvoyant according to perfectly good principles, but in an automatic way; the luciferic spirits want to deprive human beings of their free will, the possibility of doing evil.

This has to do with specific secrets of evolution. As you know, the luciferic spirits have remained stationary at other levels of evolution and bring something foreign into the normal evolutionary process. They are deeply interested in seizing hold of us and preventing us from gaining free will because they themselves have not achieved it. Free will can be gained only on earth, but the luciferic spirits want to have nothing to do with the earth; they want only Old Saturn, Old Sun and Old Moon evolution and nothing beyond this. In a sense they hate human free will. They act in a highly spiritual but automatic way—this is highly significant—and want to raise human beings to their own spiritual heights, making them spiritual but automatic. On the one hand this would create the danger that, before the consciousness soul is fully functional, human beings become spiritual automatons and sleep through the revelation that is to come, which I have characterized for you.

Ahrimanic spirits are also working against this revelation. They do not seek to make human beings particularly spiritual but to smother their awareness of their own spirituality. They want to teach people that they are really only a perfectly developed animal. Ahriman is in truth the great teacher of materialistic Darwinism. He also teaches all the technological and practical activity in earth evolution where nothing is considered valid unless it can be perceived by the senses, the desire being to have widespread technology, with people satisfying their needs for food and drink and other things in the same way as animals do, except that it is more sophisticated. To kill and obscure the human being's awareness that he is an image of the Godhead—this is the aim ahrimanic spirits are seeking to achieve by sophisticated scientific means in our age.

In earlier times it would have been of no avail for the ahrimanic spirits to obscure the truth for human beings by means of theories. The reason was that in Graeco-Latin times, and even more so before then, people still gained images through atavistic clairvoyance and it did not matter what they thought. They had their images which were like windows into the world of the spirit. Anything Ahriman might have taught them concerning their relation to animals would have had no effect on their way of life. Thinking only became a powerful process—powerful in its impotence, we might say—in our fifth post-Atlantean age, from the fifteenth century onwards. Only then did thinking become effective in taking the consciousness soul into the realm of the spirit or, indeed, preventing it from entering into the world of the spirit. Only now do we live in an age when a scientific theory may be deliberately used to deprive us of our divine nature and all experience of divine nature. This is only possible in the age of the consciousness soul. The ahrimanic spirits therefore seek to spread teachings among humanity that obscure the human being's divine origin.

This reference to the streams that go against normal and

divine human evolution may show how we must conduct our lives so that we do not sleep through the revelation that is to come. Otherwise a great danger will arise. We have to be on the alert for this, or something will develop that may be a great and real danger to earth evolution, taking the place of the significant event intended to play a momentous part in shaping the future evolution of earth.

Some spiritual beings achieve higher development because human beings develop together with them. The angels do not develop images in the human astral body as a kind of game but in order to achieve something. As the aim they have to achieve lies within earthly humanity itself, the whole matter would become a game if human beings, having reached the stage of the consciousness soul, were to deliberately ignore it. This would make it all into a game. The angels would be playing a game in the developing human astral body. It is not a game but a serious business only because it comes to realization in humanity. You will realize, therefore, that the work of the angels must always be a serious matter. Imagine what would happen behind the scenes of existence if human beings were to stay asleep and so turn the work of the angels into a game!

What if this were to happen after all? What if earthly humanity were to persist in sleeping through the momentous spiritual revelation that is to come? If humanity were to sleep through the middle part, for instance, the matter relating to religious freedom, if they were to sleep through the repetition of the Mystery of Golgotha on the etheric plane, the reappearance of the etheric Christ, or through other things, the angels would have to achieve their aim in a different way. If human beings did not, while awake, allow the angels to achieve their aim in human astral bodies, they would achieve it with the help of the physical and etheric bodies that remain in bed during sleep. This is where powers to achieve the aim would be sought. The aim not achievable with human beings who are awake, with souls awake in their etheric and physical bodies, will be achieved with the etheric and physical bodies as they lie asleep, when human beings who should be awake are outside those bodies with their ego and astral body.

Here lies the great danger for the age of the consciousness soul. It may still happen if human beings are not willing to turn to life in the spirit before the beginning of the third millennium. The third millennium begins in the year 2000, and is therefore only a short way ahead of us. It may still be necessary for the angels to achieve their aim by means of sleeping human bodies. They would have to withdraw all their work from the astral body and take it into the etheric body to do so. But then the human being would have no part in it. The work would have to be done in the etheric body when the human being is not present, for if he were present in the waking state he would obstruct it.

This gives you a general idea. But what would be the outcome if the angels were obliged to do their work without the participation of human beings, doing it in human etheric and physical bodies during sleep?

The inevitable effect on human evolution would be threefold. Firstly, something would be engendered in sleeping human bodies, when the human ego and astral body are outside, which human beings would not discover in freedom but simply find to be there when they wake up in the morning. Danger would threaten from certain instinctive perceptions connected with the mystery of birth and conception and with sexual life as a whole that are intended to be part of human nature. The danger would come from certain angels who themselves would undergo a change, which is something I cannot speak about, for it belongs to the higher secrets of initiation which may not yet be disclosed. But this much can certainly be said: the effect on human evolution would be that certain instincts belonging to the sexual life and to sexual nature would not come to clear conscious awareness in a useful way but become harmful. These instincts would not be mere aberrations but would enter into the social life, configuring it. Something would enter into people's blood as a consequence of sexual life that would above all make people go against brotherliness on earth rather than develop brotherliness. This would be a matter of instinct.

A crucial time will come when the path to the right may be taken—which demands wakefulness—or the path to the left, where people sleep. Instincts of a truly horrific nature would then develop.

What do you suppose scientific experts will say when such instincts emerge? They will consider them a natural and inevitable development in human evolution. Light cannot be shed on such matters by ordinary science, for scientific reasoning can be used to explain why people become angels or devils. In either case one thing always follows from another—the great wisdom of causality! Scientists will be completely blind to the event of which I have spoken, for they will simply consider it to be a natural necessity that people turn into half devils because of their sexual instincts. There can be no scientific explanation, for anything and everything can always be explained in science. The fact is that such things can only be understood by spiritual insight that goes beyond the sphere of the senses.

Secondly, this work, which also brings changes for the

angels, will cause humanity to gain instinctive knowledge of some medicines, but harmful knowledge of them. Everything connected with medicine will make great advances in the materialistic sense. People will gain instinctive insight into the medicinal properties of some substances and techniques and this will cause tremendous damage but will be said to be beneficial. Pathological changes will be called normal, for people will find that this leads to a certain technique that pleases them. They will actually like things that in a certain way take humanity into an unhealthy state. Knowledge of the medicinal powers of certain processes and techniques will increase but this will lead into very harmful channels. Out of certain instincts people will know the kind of diseases which can be produced by specific substances and techniques, and they will be able to arrange matters entirely to suit their egotistical purposes, to provoke diseases or not to provoke them.

Thirdly, humanity will get to know specific powers that enable it to unleash tremendous mechanical forces in the world by means of quite simple manipulations—bringing certain wave-lengths into harmony. They will instinctively come to realize that it is possible to exercise some degree of mental control over mechanics. This will take the whole of technology along disastrous channels, a state of affairs, however, that will serve human egotism extremely well and please people.

Here we gain clear insight into the evolution of existence, and we perceive a conception of life that can really only be properly appreciated by those who understand that we shall never be clear about these things if we take an unspiritual view of life. People with an unspiritual view of life would not be able to perceive that an approach to medicine was causing harm to humanity, that sexual instincts were going desperately astray, that a terrible hustle and bustle of purely mechanistic activity was arising as forces of nature were utilized through powers of the mind. They would not realize that this meant deviation from the true path, just as someone who is asleep cannot see the thief who comes to rob him; the incident would pass him by; at most he would realize what had happened later, after he had woken up. But it would be a terrible awakening for humanity. People would delight in the instinctive broadening of their knowledge of certain processes and substances; they would gain a certain satisfaction in the pursuit of sexual aberrations, regarding them as evidence of an advanced development of more than human qualities, lack of prejudice and broad-mindedness. In some respects ugliness would be considered beauty and beauty ugliness. None of this would be noticed for it would be taken for natural necessity. It would, however, be a deviation from the path laid down for humanity in the individual nature given to human beings.

I think if we develop a feeling for the way the science of the spirit enters into our attitudes of mind we can also be truly serious in our approach to truths like those presented today, and gain from them what really should be gained from the whole of this science: to recognize a certain obligation, certain responsibilities in life. Whatever our role in life and in the world, it is important that we have the thought: everything we do must be imbued with and illumined by anthroposophical awareness. We then contribute something to the true advancement of human evolution.

It would be entirely wrong to believe that the true science of the spirit, approached in a serious and worthy mood, could ever divert us from the necessary practical involvement in life. The true science of the spirit makes us wake up with regard to such matters as I have spoken of today.

3.5

These three extracts have been included as an indication of how Rudolf Steiner wished to repudiate Freud's theories of infant sexuality. He was also critical of psychoanalysis as a therapy on account of its separating the interconnection of body and soul and ignoring the spirit. The background to these lectures is, however, of special interest here. Even critics of Steiner have observed that as a spiritual teacher he was exemplary in his dealings with the opposite sex (unlike certain 'gurus'), but in 1915 there arose precisely that accusation of emotional interference of a kind that has darkened other movements. Alice Sprengel was a pupil of Steiner's who had acted the part of Theodora in his first Mystery Drama. When in 1914 Steiner got married to his co-worker Marie von Sivers, Alice Sprengel accused him of having originally promised to marry her, a fact which he completely denied. It seems that she had deluded herself into misinterpreting his general warmth and friendliness to all, in particular his handshakes. She was aided in her accusations by Heinrich Goesch, a married man who had evidently become involved with her, who was also a student of Freud's (then new) psychoanalytic theories. There was an uproar within the newly founded Anthroposophical Society, and members voted to expel Alice Sprengel, Goesch and his wife Gertrud, who seems to have supported her husband. Alice Sprengel was apparently a deeply disturbed woman who had undergone 'unusual suffering' in childhood (possibly sexual abuse). She later went on to join the OTO (Ordo Templi Orientis), which by then had developed practices involving sexual magical rituals. In hindsight matters could perhaps have been handled differently, but this was 1915.

Neither Rudolf nor Marie Steiner were part of the vote to exclude her, and Marie Steiner went on to offer her financial assistance. The full background with correspondence can be read in the volume Community Life, Inner Development, Sexuality and the Spiritual Teacher *(see 'Sources').*

The second extract shows that Rudolf Steiner felt it was very important to stress the separation of the sexual-emotional life from any mystical tendencies. He wanted his listeners to be aware of the delusions that can arise around a spiritual teacher—and thus gave this series of lectures and addresses, parts of which are included here. It is probably the only place where he addressed the theme of sexuality as fully as he does—though not what today would be considered as full. In the third extract he attempts to show how human sexuality has 'descended' so to speak in human evolution. His criticism of Freudian psychoanalysis may sound harsh but it is worth remembering that other models of human psychology exist today, and many aspects of Freudian theory have been questioned.

3.5.1 Methods and rationale of Freudian psychoanalysis

First of all, and from a very specific point of view, I would like to address the question of what we are really being confronted with in the Goesch-Sprengel case. In recent lectures 1 have often said that it is important to arrive at the appropriate perspective from which to try to resolve any given issue. How, then, can we arrive at the right perspective on this particular matter through objective study of the case?

In order to deal with a case like this objectively, we must first of all remove it from its personal context and insert it into a larger one. If, as I believe, this larger context turns out to be what is most important for our anthroposophical movement, we will find ourselves obliged to study this case to learn from it and for the sake of spiritual science itself. And in fact there is a larger context to the case, as will become apparent if we look at Dr Goesch's letter of 19 August 1915 with an eye to his main motives and arguments.

Since you have important deliberations ahead of you, I will not detain you too long, but will only select a few essential points for your consideration. The first is Dr Goesch's claim that promises have not been kept. If you listened to the letter carefully, you will have noticed that the emphasis in his reproach is not on the alleged making and not keeping of promises. His primary accusation is that I looked for and systematically applied a means of making promises to members and not keeping them, and that once the members noticed that these promises were not being kept they were put into a state of mind that forced them into a particular relationship to the one who had made and not kept the promises. As a result, forces accumulated in their souls that eventually made them lose their sound judgement.

So the first hypothesis Dr Goesch presents is that systematic attempts were made to stifle the members' good sense, that deliberately making and breaking promises was a means of dulling their normal state of consciousness, resulting in a kind of stupefaction that turned them into zombies. That is the first point his letter addresses.

His second point has to do with one of the means of carrying this out. To put it briefly, through handshakes and friendly conversations and the like I am supposed to have initiated a kind of contact with members that was suited, because of its very nature and the influence it allowed me to exert, to bringing about the above-mentioned effect on their souls.

A third thing we must keep in mind as a recurrent theme running through Dr Goesch's whole letter is the nature of his relationship to Miss Sprengel. We could add to these three points, but let us deal with them first.

To begin with, how does Dr Goesch manage to construct such a systematic theory, based on his first two points, about how steps were taken to undermine the members' state of consciousness? We need to go into this thoroughly and try to find out where it comes from. In Dr Goesch's case, we are led to his long involvement with Dr Freud's so-called theory of psychoanalysis.[35] If you study this theory, you will begin to see that it is intimately related to how the pathological picture presented in the letter develops. Certain connections can be drawn between this pathological picture, as it relates to Dr Goesch's first two points, and his involvement with the Freudian psychoanalytic point of view.

Of course, I am not in a position to give you a comprehensive picture of Freudian psychoanalytic theory in brief— my intent is only to present a few points that will help clarify the Goesch-Sprengel case. However, in a certain sense I do feel qualified to talk about psychoanalysis, because in my earlier years I was friends with one of the medical experts involved in its very beginnings.[36] This person eventually abandoned the theory of psychoanalysis after it degenerated later on in Freud's life. In any case, please do not take what I am going to say now as a comprehensive characterization of Freudian theory; I only want to highlight a few points.

Freudian psychoanalysts start from the assumption that an unconscious inner life exists alongside our conscious soul-activity—that is, in addition to the soul-activity we are conscious of, there is also an unconscious inner life we are usually not aware of. An important component of psychoanalysis is the doctrine that certain experiences people have in the course of their life can make impressions on them, but these impressions disappear from their conscious awareness and work on in their subconscious. According to the psychoanalysts, we do not necessarily become fully conscious of these experiences before they sink down into the unconscious—for example, something can make an impression on a person during childhood without ever coming to full consciousness, and still have such an effect on that person's psyche that it sinks down into the unconscious and goes on working there. Its effects are lasting, and in some cases lead to psychological disorders later on. I am skipping a lot of links in the chain of reasoning and jumping right to the outcome of the whole process. In other words, we are to imagine in the soul's subconscious depths a kind of island of childhood and youthful experiences gone rampant. Through questioning during psychoanalysis, these subconscious proliferating islands in the soul can be lifted up into consciousness and incorporated into the structure of conscious awareness. In the process, the person in question can be cured of psychological defects in that particular area.

During the early years of the psychoanalytic movement, it was the practice of Dr Breuer in particular to carry out this questioning with the patient under hypnosis. Later on, this practice was discontinued, and now the Freudian school conducts this analysis with the patient in a normal waking state of consciousness. In any case, the underlying assumption is that there are unhealthy, proliferating islands present in the psyche below the level of consciousness.

This psychoanalytic outlook has gradually spread to incorporate and try to explain all kinds of phenomena of ordinary life, particularly with regard to how they appear in people's dreams. As I already explained once in a lecture to our friends in another city, it is at this point that the Freudian school really goes out on a limb in saying that unfulfilled desires play a primary role in dreams.[37] Freudians say that it is typical for people to experience unfulfilled desires in their dreams, desires that cannot be satisfied in real life. It can sometimes happen—and from the point of view of psycho-analytic theorists it is significant when it does—that one of these desires present on an unconscious island in the psyche is lifted up in a dream and reveals in disguised form an impulse that had an effect on the person in question during his or her childhood.

Please note the peculiarity of this train of thought. It is assumed that as young boys or girls people have experiences that sink down into the subconscious and work on as fantasy experiences, clouding their consciousness. The pattern, then, is this: experiences of waking life are repressed and continue to work on the subconscious, leading to a weakened state of consciousness. This is exactly the same pattern Dr Goesch constructs with regard to promises being given and broken and working on in the subconscious—all with the intention to create the same effect in the subconscious as the 'islands' in Freudian psychoanalytic theory. According to Dr Goesch, this was done cunningly and deliberately and resulted in a state of stupefaction analogous to what occurs when experiences of waking life have sunk into the sub-conscious and are brought up again in a dream.

Psychoanalytic theory is a very tricky business, and if you dwell on it long enough, it gives rise to certain forms of thought that spread and affect all your thinking. As you can see, this has something to do with why Dr Goesch came up with such a crazy idea.

In addition, as I have said before, the concept of physical contact plays an important part. I am now going to read certain passages from one of Prof. Freud's books, a collection of essays from the Freudian journal *Imago*, and I ask you to pay close attention to them.[38] But I must precede with something else concerning the Goesch-Sprengel case. Those of you who have known Miss Sprengel for some time will recall that she was always very concerned about protecting herself from other people's influence on her aura—she lived in horror of having to shake hands and things like that. Even before Dr Goesch arrived on the scene, she had already got the idea that shaking hands is a criminal act in our esoteric circles. The following incident is absolutely typical. I had business to do in Dr Schmiedel's laboratory and happened to meet Miss Sprengel there. I extended my hand to her, which gave her grounds for saying, 'That's how he always does it— he does whatever he wants to you and then shakes hands, and then you forget all about it.' There you have the origin of that theory about handshaking. Yesterday you all heard what this theory became in Miss Sprengel's confused mind with the help of Dr Goesch. He contributed his understanding of Freud's theories and combined things systematically with Freudian ideas.

The following passage is from page 29 of the above-mentioned book by Freud:

The principal characteristic of the psychological con-stellation which becomes fixed in this way is what might be described as the subject's ambivalent attitude (to borrow the apt term coined by Bleuler) towards a single object, or rather towards one act in connection with that object. He is constantly wishing to perform this act (the touching), [and looks on it as his supreme enjoyment, but he must not perform it] and detests it as well. The conflict between these two currents cannot be promptly settled because—there is no other way of putting it— they are localized in the subject's mind in such a manner that they cannot come up against each other. The prohibition is noisily conscious, while the persistent desire to touch is unconscious and the subject knows nothing of it. If it were not for this psychological factor, an ambivalence like this could neither last so long nor lead to such consequences.

This is followed by a long discussion of the role fear of physical contact plays in cases of neurosis:

In our clinical history of a case we have insisted that the imposition of the prohibition in very early childhood is the determining point; a similar importance attaches in the subsequent developments to the mechanism of repression at the same early age. As a result of the repression which has been enforced and which involves a loss of memory—an amnesia—the motives for the prohibition (which is conscious) remain unknown; and all attempts at disposing of it by intellectual processes must fail, since they cannot find any base of attack. The prohibition owes its strength and its obsessive character precisely to its unconscious opponent, the concealed and undiminished desire—that is to say, to an internal necessity inaccessible to conscious inspection. The ease with which the prohibition can be transferred and extended reflects a process which falls in with the unconscious desire and is greatly facilitated by the psychological conditions that prevail in the unconscious. The instinctual desire is constantly shifting in order to escape from the impasse and endeavours to find substitutes—substitute objects and substitute acts—in place of the prohibited ones. In consequence of this, the prohibition itself shifts about as well, and extends to any new aims which the forbidden impulse may adopt. Any fresh advance made by the repressed libido is answered by a fresh sharpening of the prohibition. The mutual inhibition of the two conflicting forces produces a need for discharge, for reducing the prevailing tension; and to this may be attributed the reason for the performance of obsessive acts. In the case of a neurosis these are clearly compromise actions: from one point of view they are evidences of remorse, efforts at expiation, and so on, while on the other hand they are at the same time substitutive acts to compensate the instinct for what has been prohibited. It is a law of neurotic illness that these obsessive acts fall more and more under the sway of the instinct and approach nearer and nearer to the activity which was originally prohibited.

Considering the obsessions involved in fear of physical contact, you can well imagine how it would have been if Miss Sprengel, as a person suffering from this fear, had ever been seen by a psychoanalyst who, in line with usual psychoanalytic practice, would have questioned her about her fear of contact and tried to discover what caused it.

A third factor I want to emphasize is the relationship of Miss Sprengel to Dr Goesch. According to psychoanalytic theory, this relationship would of course be characterized by the presence of repressed erotic thoughts. I mean that quite objectively . . . [39]

At this point, my friends, we must look a bit more closely at the whole system of psychoanalysis. As I have just outlined for you, psychoanalysis lifts up into consciousness certain 'islands' in the unconscious psyche, and it assumes that the majority of these islands are sexual in nature. The psychoanalyst's task, then, is to reach down to the level of these early experiences that have sunk into the subconscious and lift them up again for purposes of healing. According to Freudian theory, healing is brought about by lifting hidden sexual complexes up from the depths of the subconscious and making the person aware of them again. Whether this method is very successful is a matter of much discussion in books on the subject.

As you can see, psychoanalysts' thinking is often coloured by an underlying pervasive sexuality, and this is taken to extremes when psychoanalysis is applied to any and all possible phenomena of human life. For example, Freud and his disciples go so far as to interpret myths and legends psychoanalytically, tracing them to repressed sexuality. Consider, for example, how they interpret the story of Oedipus.[40] In brief, the content of this legend is that Oedipus is led to kill his father and marry his mother. When psychoanalysts ask what this story is based on, they conclude that such things always rest on unconscious, repressed sexual complexes usually involving sexual experiences in earliest childhood. The Freudians are firmly convinced that a child's relationship to his or her father and mother is a sexual one right from birth, so if the child is a boy, he must be unconsciously in love with his mother and thus unconsciously or subconsciously jealous of his father.

At this point, my friends, we might be tempted to say that these psychoanalysts, if they actually believe in their own theory, should apply it to themselves first and foremost, and admit that their own destiny and outlook stem from an excess of repressed sexual processes experienced in childhood. Freud and his disciples should apply this theory to themselves first. They derive the Oedipus legend, for instance, from their assumption that most little boys have an illicit emotional relationship to their mother right from birth, and are thus jealous of their father. Thus, the boys' father becomes their enemy and works on as such in their troubled imagination. Later, however, they realize rationally that this relationship to their mother is not permissible, and so it is repressed and becomes subconscious. The boys then live out their lives without becoming aware of their forbidden relationship to their mother and their adversarial relationship to their father, whom they experience as a rival.

According to psychoanalytic theory, then, what we need to do in cases of defective psyches is to look for psychological complexes, and we will find that if these are lifted up into consciousness a cure can be effected. It is a pity that I cannot present these things in greater detail, but I will try to give you as exact an outline of them as possible. On page 16 of the above-mentioned book, for instance, you can read the following:

> There has been little opportunity in the preceding pages for showing how new light can be thrown upon the facts of social psychology by the adoption of a psychoanalytic method of approach: for the horror of incest displayed by savages has long been recognized as such and stands in need of no further interpretation.[41]

This essay explains why primitive peoples so strictly enforce the ban on marrying one's mother or sister and why relationships of this type are punished. 'Incest' is love for a blood-relative, and one of the first essays in this book is entitled 'The Horror of Incest'. This fear is explained by assuming the existence of a tendency to incest on the part of each male individual in the form of a forbidden relationship to his mother.

> All that I have been able to add to our understanding of it is to emphasize the fact that it is essentially an infantile feature [that is, primitive people retain this for a lifetime, while in civilized children it is repressed into the sub-conscious] and that it reveals a striking agreement with the mental life of neurotic patients. Psychoanalysis has taught us that a boy's earliest choice of objects for his love is incestuous and that those objects are forbidden ones—his mother and his sister. We have learnt, too, the manner in which, as he grows up, he liberates himself from this incestuous attraction. A neurotic, on the other hand, invariably exhibits some degree of psychical infantilism. He has either failed to get free from the psychosexual conditions that prevailed in his childhood or he has returned to them—two possibilities which may be summed up as developmental inhibition and regression. Thus incestuous fixations of libido continue to play (or begin once more to play) the principal part in his unconscious mental life. We have arrived at the point of regarding a child's relation to his parents, dominated as it is by incestuous longings, as the nuclear complex of neurosis.

Thus, according to psychoanalytic theory, the central complex involved in neurosis is a boy's forbidden sexual attraction for his mother and sister.

This revelation of the importance of incest in neurosis is naturally received with universal scepticism by adults and normal people. Similar expressions of disbelief, for instance, inevitably greet the writings of Otto Rank,[42] which have brought more and more evidence to show the extent to which the interest of creative writers centres on the theme of incest and how the same theme, in countless variations and distortions, provides the subject-matter of poetry. We are driven to believe that this rejection is principally a product of the distaste which human beings feel for their early incestuous wishes, now overtaken by repression. It is therefore of no small importance that we are able to show that these same incestuous wishes, which are later destined to become unconscious, are still regarded by savage peoples as immediate perils against which the most severe measures of defence must be enforced.

From this point of departure, an atmosphere of sexuality spreads until it pervades the psychoanalysts' whole field of activity. Their whole life is spent working with ideas about sexuality. That is why psychoanalysis has been the biggest contributing factor in making an unbelievable mockery of something quite natural in human life. This has crept into our life gradually, without people noticing it. I can sympathize deeply with an old gentleman by the name of Moritz Benedikt (who spent his life trying to bring morality into medicine) when he says that if you look around, you will find that the physicians of 30 years ago knew less about certain sexual abnormalities than 18-year-old girls in boarding school do today.[43] This is the truth, and you can really empathize with this man. I mention it in particular because it is really extremely important to regard certain processes in children's lives as simply natural, without having to see them in terms of sexuality right away.

Nowadays, these complicated psychoanalytic theories lead us to label a lot of what children do as sexually deviant, although most of it is totally innocent. In most cases, it would be enough to regard these things as nothing more than childish mischievousness that could be quite adequately treated with a couple of smacks on a certain part of the anatomy. The worst possible way of dealing with it, however, is to talk a lot about these things, especially with the children themselves, and to put all kinds of theoretical ideas in their heads. It is hard enough to talk about these things with grown-ups with any degree of clarity. Unfortunately for people who are often called upon to provide counselling, parents frequently come with all kinds of complaints, including some really silly ones about how their children suffer from sexual deviance. Their only basis for these complaints is that the children scratch themselves. Now, there is no more sexuality involved in scratching yourself anywhere else than there is in scratching your arm. Dr Freud, however, upholds the idea that any scratching or touching, or even a baby sucking a dummy, is a sexual activity. He spreads a mantle of sexuality over all aspects of human life.

It would be good for us to look more closely at Freudian psychoanalysis in order to become aware of the excesses of materialistic science, specifically of those of psychoanalysis in seeing everything in terms of sexuality. In a book introduced by Dr Freud, the Hungarian psychoanalyst Ferenczi writes about the case of a five-year-old boy named Arpad.[44] There is no doubt in his mind as to the sources of Arpad's interest in the goings-on in the chicken run:

The continual sexual activity between the cock and hens, the laying of eggs and the hatching out of the young brood gratified his sexual curiosity, the real object of which was human family life. He showed that he had formed his own choice of sexual objects on the model of life in the hen-run, for he said one day to the neighbour's wife: 'I'll marry you and your sister and my three cousins and the cook; no, not the cook, I'll marry my mother instead.'[45]

We could wish for a return of the days when it was possible to hear children say things like this without immediately having to resort to such awkward sexual explanations. I can only touch on this subject today, but I will discuss it at greater length sometime in the near future in order to reassure all you fathers and mothers.[46] But of course, Freud's theory, which is spreading widely without people noticing it, is only a symptom of a worldwide tendency. And when parents come with the complaint that their four or five-year-old sons or daughters are suffering from sexual deviance, in most cases the appropriate response is, 'The only deviant thing in this case is your way of thinking about it!' In most instances, that is really what's wrong.

My intention in telling you all this has been to point out the kind of atmosphere Freudian psychoanalysis is swimming in. I am well aware that the Freudians would take issue with this brief characterization. But we are fully justified in saying that psychoanalysis as a whole is positively dripping with these psychosexual things, as its professional literature reveals.

Suppose the assumption that psychosexual islands exist in the human subconscious actually proves to be true in the case of a certain individual. A Freudian theorist might subject that

person to questioning and be able to add a new case history
to the annals of Freudian psychoanalytic theory. In the case
concerning us, Dr Goesch might have undertaken this line of
questioning and made some discoveries among those
psychosexual islands that would have served to verify Freud's
theories. But to do that, Dr Goesch would have needed to be
stronger in his own soul. As it was, however, he succumbed
to a certain type of relationship to his new lady friend. The
material in our possession supplies ample evidence of this
relationship and will allow anyone who applies it in the right
way to describe their relationship with clinical, objective
precision.

What, then, was actually going on in the Goesch-Sprengel
case? Dr Goesch could not really function as a psychoanalyst,
because to do that his relationship to Miss Sprengel would
have had to be an objective one like that of a doctor to a
patient. Her influence on him was too overwhelming, however, and thus his involvement in the examination was not
fully conscious and objective. In Freudian terms, everything
at work in the psyche of his friend, the 'keeper of the seal',[47]
came out, but since it sank down into Dr Goesch's unconscious, it was masked by the whole theory that came to light
in his letter.

The Goesch-Sprengel case grew out of one of the greatest
mistakes and worst materialistic theories of our time, and we
can only deal with it by realizing that both people involved
threw a mantle of secrecy over their human, all-too-human
relationships. In essence, this consisted of shrouding their
relationship in Freudian psychoanalytic theories, as the
documents very clearly reveal.

When we attempt to help people who come to us in such a
confused psychological state, they are often fawning,

enthusiastic supporters to begin with, but later on their adulation changes into enmity. That, too, can be explained in psychoanalytic terms. However, our most urgent concern at the moment is our relationship to the rest of the world. Just as we are now experiencing hostility coming from the direction of psychoanalysis, steeped as it is in sexuality, we can expect to encounter at any moment new opposition from all kinds of aberrations resulting from other all-too-human impulses.

3.5.2 *The concept of love and mysticism*

Let us continue with the theme we have been considering for the past few days and begin by asking the question 'How old is love?' There is no doubt in my mind that the great majority of people with their rather superficial way of looking at things would immediately respond that love is as old as the human race, of course. However, anyone who recognizes cultural history as being imbued with spiritual impulses, and who therefore tries to deal with such issues concretely instead of in vague generalities, would answer quite differently. Love, my friends, is seven hundred years old at the most!

Nowhere in ancient Greek and Roman prose or poetry will you find anything resembling our modern idea of love. And if you read Plutarch, for instance, you will find the two concepts of Venus and Amor very clearly differentiated.[48] Love as the subject of so much lyrical eloquence in literature, and especially in poetry, is no more than six or seven hundred years old. Our modern notion of love—what love means to us today and how that is instilled in people—has played a part in the human heart and mind only for the past six or seven centuries. Before that, people did not have the same idea of love; they did not speak about it in any even remotely similar way.

This should not come as a surprise to you, not even on a theoretical or epistemological level. The objection that human beings have always made a practice of loving does not hold good; that would be like saying that if the earth revolves around the sun, as the Copernican view claims, then it must have been doing so even during Roman, Greek and Egyptian times—in fact, as long as it has been in existence. Of course that's true, but the people of those times did not refer to the Copernican system.

Similarly, it is also not valid to object that what is expressed in the idea of love must have existed before the concept itself was there. Of course, the facts and phenomena of loving have always been an identifiable facet of human life, but people have not always talked about them. We have come a long way in the past six or seven hundred years in that respect; in fact, we have come so far that love occupies a central position in many people's view of life. And not only that, we now have a scientific theory, the theory of psychoanalysis, which is positively swimming in the most vulgar concepts of love, as I have shown. This is an evolutionary tendency that anthroposophists in particular are called upon to resist and to transform by fostering a spiritual-scientific philosophy of life.

Many of you may be aware that I described these same things quite precisely from a historical perspective in some earlier lectures, so I would be surprised if you were all taken aback by my statement that our idea of love is only six or seven hundred years old.[49] In any case, the idea of love has gradually crept into all kinds of philosophical concepts during the past few hundred years, as is revoltingly evident in psychoanalysis. It would take a long time to get to the bottom of all this, but I hope these more or less aphoristic remarks will give you some clues.

As an example, let us consider a contemporary thinker who is totally immersed in modern cultural concepts—in other words, someone who cannot overcome his supposed insight that outer sensory-physical reality is all we can reasonably talk about. I have already introduced Fritz Mauthner to you as a very sincere representative of this type of person.[50] Mauthner is a linguistic critic and the author of a philosophical dictionary. This puts him in a very strange position in that it makes him aware of the fact that the word 'mysticism' has existed down through the ages—as a linguistic critic, he naturally wants to know what stands behind both the word itself and actual mystical aspirations.

My friends, just consider how much reading material we have to struggle through to understand that particular relationship of the human soul to supersensory worlds that deserves the name 'mysticism'. Consider, too, how very seriously we have to take any explanations, such as those in *Knowledge of the Higher Worlds*, if we want to understand the inner attitude needed in order to face the spiritual world as a mystic—that is, as a soul at one with the spiritual pulse and flow of higher worlds. We can only really say what mysticism is in the modern sense of the word when we have engaged in serious reflection such as that in *Knowledge of the Higher Worlds*. In other words, we have to at least study that book thoroughly and attentively a couple of times.

However, Mauthner is not only honest, he is also thorough, and so he wonders if it is actually true that human souls have never experienced anything like mysticism. After all, people have always talked about it. What was it, then, that induced them to speak about mysticism?

If you try to find how Mauthner discovers what underlies mysticism, the most you can say after having read the entry on mysticism in his dictionary is that he keeps going around in circles. Everything in this article revolves around words and definitions of words. But since I was interested in finding out how Mauthner, in his own way, attempts to get at what is behind mysticism, I looked it up in his dictionary to see what could be found there [gap in the stenographic record].

So I looked up not only his entry on mysticism but also the one on love. I found the article on love to be one of his best, and very well written. It is actually very nice. Mauthner first mentions Spinoza's definition of love and Schopenhauer's brief and heavy-handed definition, and then he explains that it is necessary to distinguish between mere eroticism, which is strictly physical and confined to sexuality, and real love on a soul level. Mauthner admits all that, and even goes on to say something as elevated as this:[51]

> I believe that the one-sided intellectual geniuses have seldom, if ever, had any understanding of love in its highest degree, of feelings of love taken to pathological extremes. They have not experienced it personally and have only tried to categorize the descriptions of poets.

That is, the philosophers did not know much about love except what they looked up in books of poetry.

> I believe that love in its ultimate degree has been experienced and described only by artists (approximately since the time of Petrarch), and that it entered common parlance through the power of imitation or fashion and captured the imagination of readers for six hundred years, and is now in the process of being replaced by another fashion. Although the ultimate degree of love is as rare as a great artistic creation or the

kind of religious union with God that St Francis may have experienced, still the whole world babbles on about religion, art and love. What they mean by all this are mere substitutes for emotions that perhaps one person in a million has actually experienced.

Fair enough!

The ultimate degree of love, whose existence I do not deny, is really something of a miracle—and people have also tried to explain miracles as pathological phenomena. In the most unlikely event that both sexual partners experience the highest degree of love, a miracle takes place in defiance of all the laws of nature: each one lifts the other and both float above the earth. Archimedes' principle is, or appears to be, negated. Whether in happiness or in death, the longing of mysticism is fulfilled.

There you have it. For someone like Mauthner, steeped in modern materialistic philosophy, the emotion of love is the only way human beings can experience the feelings 'deranged' mystics experience in their relationship to spiritual things. 'Whether in happiness or in death, the longing of mysticism is fulfilled' is a remarkably honest sentence coming from someone who has lost all connection to the spiritual world. Mauthner continues:

The well-known feeling that leads us to call our sexual partners 'lovers' runs through so-called love in all its various degrees. And we describe our very subjective experience through the unwarranted use of the corresponding verb 'to love'. The attempt to find an objective noun, namely the word 'love' to describe this experience, met with such success that people have persuaded themselves that the experience itself is as common as the word 'love' has become.

As you can see, when the modern materialistic world tries to formulate a concept of mysticism out of its own fundamental impulses, it is forced to conclude that what mystics dream of can only be found in the emotion of love in the real world; that is, everything spiritual is dragged down into a refined version of eroticism.

It is typical, for instance, that Mauthner brings up the particular way in which a woman friend of Nietzsche's, the author Lou Andreas-Salomé,[52] describes Nietzsche's intellect as a type of refined eroticism.[53] It is interesting, too, how Mauthner reacts to her portrayal of Nietzsche. He says:

> Recently, after so many attempts by men, a woman, Friedrich Nietzsche's friend Lou Andreas-Salomé, has also tried to formulate a philosophy of love in her excellent book on Nietzsche, which won her the hatred of the entire Nietzsche clan. She is very subtle in her expositions, but bold enough to refuse to accept fidelity as an attribute of love, and she forges a link between the artist's fantasy and that of lovers ('Eroticism', p. 25). She too, however, intellectualizes the act to such an extent that there seems to be no conceptual distinction between sensuality and the intellectual phenomena accompanying it.

In other words, then, from the way men and women express themselves, we see that nowadays, even in our thinking, we have to replace our relationship to the spiritual world with the eroticism throbbing in our souls—a more or less refined eroticism, depending on the character of the individual in question. This all has to do with the fundamental materialistic tendency of our times, which also leads to untruthfulness when people are not honest enough to admit that all they know about mysticism is the aspect that is identical to eroticism. Untruthfulness emerges when these people talk about eroticism but conceal it behind a veil of mystical concepts. Materialists who freely admit that they see nothing but eroticism in all of mysticism are actually much more honest than people who take eroticism as their starting point but hide it behind mystical formulas as they clamber up to the very highest worlds. Sometimes you can almost see the ladders they are using to scramble up to the very highest planes of existence in order to have a mystical cover-up for something that is actually nothing more than eroticism. On the one hand, then, we have the theoretical linking of mysticism to eroticism, and on the other hand the tendency of our modern times to sink down into eroticism and drag all kinds of murky, misunderstood mysticism into it.

Some time ago I challenged you to work on eradicating the mystical eccentricities that come about through the kind of mingling of spheres I described, so that people who are well able to recognize the noble character of spirituality will once again be able to rise to the perspective needed to speak about spirituality where spirituality is actually present, without clothing subjective emotions in spiritual forms. In making this appeal, I hoped to create some degree of clarity in these matters within the Anthroposophical Society, so that clear thinking might prevail. Time alone will tell whether we will actually be able to accomplish this.

In former times (and in fact until quite recently, as I pointed out yesterday), a much more radical means was used to safeguard the basic requirements of any kind of spiritual-scientific society. It was a simple matter of excluding one entire gender, half of humanity, so that the other half would be spared the dangers inherent in mixing elevated spiritual concepts with thoughts of natural human activity on the physical plane. Thinking about spiritual matters belongs to the spiritual world. We must come to the healthy realization that it is much worse to talk about certain aspects of natural human interaction in mystical formulas that do not belong to this natural level than it is to call these things honestly by name and admit that this aspect belongs to the physical plane and must remain there.

Schopenhauer, in his singularly heavy-handed fashion, characterized love as follows: 'The sum total of the current generation's love affairs are thus the human race's "earnest *meditatio compositionis generationis futurae, e qua iterum pendent innumerae generations*"'—the earnest meditation of the human race as a whole on the composition of generations to come, on which in turn countless generations depend.[54] Well, that is Schopenhauer's opinion, not mine! It is a terrible thing to see people deny the rightful place of such urges and disguise them by saying, for example, that they are obliged to do what they do so that an extremely important individuality can incarnate. That is really an abomination in the eyes of someone trying to practise mysticism in all earnestness and dignity.

We must also take into account the fact that mysticism is not intended as an excuse for laziness on our part. That is what it becomes, however, when healthy concepts are replaced by unhealthy ones in the name of mysticism. Here on the physical plane, people are supposed to make their mark through good will and work—real hard work. If they prefer to gain recognition under false pretences rather than on the merits of their work, and demand special treatment by virtue of being the reincarnation of somebody or other, then they are using mysticism as an excuse. They want to be recognized as someone special without doing a thing. This is a very trivial and vulgarized way of looking at the matter.

If we are making every effort, as indeed we must nowadays, to foster spiritual science openly in the presence of both sexes, the old compulsory bans must be replaced by a serious and dignified attitude on the part of both men and women as they seek to acquire knowledge of the higher worlds. We must succeed in eliminating from this search all the fantasies bound up with our lower human drives. Only then will we be able to prevent the proliferation of errors originating in the illusions of individuals prone to mystical laziness. Mysticism, my friends, does not ask us to become lazier than the people out there who care nothing about it. If anything, it requires us to be more diligent than they are. And mystical morality cannot mean sinking below the moral level of other human beings; rather we must advance beyond it. If we do not make a serious effort to eradicate anything resembling 'Sprengelism', as I would like to call it, from our Society, we will make no progress.

3.5.3 The descent of human sexuality and the critique of Freudian psychoanalysis

In the past few days we have been looking at the theory of psychoanalysis, a singularly revolting philosophy of life. In this instance, we can use this term freely without being in the least subjective. As we said, it is not its point of departure that makes psychoanalysis revolting—in fact, its starting point

could equally well lead to correct conclusions if applied
properly. It becomes revolting because of the way the people
involved with it intrude their personal feelings and emotions.
The fact that it has incorporated personal and subjective
aspects is the reason why psychoanalytic theory is positively
dripping with sexuality, as I put it before.

However, if people who are aware of the principle of first
discovering the right perspective became acquainted with the
psychoanalytic theory's point of departure and proceeded
from there, the results would be quite different. They might
incorporate certain materialistic affectations into psychoanalytic theory to begin with, but they would soon be forced
to adopt purer and nobler means of understanding simply
through having made the distinction between the conscious
and the unconscious mind. They would realize that dragging
in points of view of the sort we mentioned before is not
objective but a sign of arbitrary emotions belonging to subjective human nature.

The most significant aspect of any true study is that it tends
to lead us far beyond our original point of departure. Rather
than incorporating our own subjective impulses into the
subject, we are guided and spurred on by the subject itself.
Eventually, every true student becomes aware of how truly
necessary this principle is. It is indispensable in making any
spiritual-scientific world-view into a reality and equally
indispensable to the structure of a society in which such a
world-view is to be fostered. We must finally realize that we
have to take anthroposophy seriously and give it the respect it
deserves. That is, we must not incorporate previous subjective habits into things belonging to our spiritual-scientific
philosophy, but must rather let ourselves be guided by what
that philosophy requires. For example, in everyday life

someone may be in the habit of always arriving late instead of at the specified time. In ordinary bourgeois life that habit may be merely unpleasant or less than advantageous for that person's advancement, but in our anthroposophical movement the whole way we deal with spiritual-scientific truths ought to make that kind of behaviour an inner impossibility except in cases of dire necessity.

In the past few days, we have talked a lot about dignity— not only the essential dignity of spiritual science itself, but also the dignity of our own interactions within the Society. We saw how important it is for us to spend time together as members among ourselves, with no one else present. Of course, making sure we arrive on time is a superficial thing, but in the past few days people have still been coming late, even though the lectures started at twenty past six. If we carry on like that, my friends, we will never even be able to begin to realize the ideal of our Society. In the somewhat attenuated circumstances that come about when we cannot be sure that members will not continue to arrive once we have begun, we will never be able to rule out the possibility of having uninvited guests in our midst. It is simply inconsiderate to come late to a Society function when the Society needs to make sure that everyone present is actually a member; that is, when some of us have to go to the extra effort of keeping an eye on the people entering until all members are present. When the people standing at the door have come in, we need to be able to shut the doors and know that everyone is here.

It should certainly not be necessary to make a special point of talking about things like this, but in spiritual science we have to be guided by the concept of symptomatology, which simply means that any being tends to act the same way in important instances as it does in less significant ones. People who do not even manage to arrive on time for meetings will also not be able to act out of the requisite sense of responsibility when it comes to something important. A great deal of the damage that has become so blatantly evident lately has come about because people were not particular enough about certain things. It is really important for us to conduct the practical affairs of anthroposophy with the conscientious exactitude I just mentioned. We have seen an example of how we as members of a spiritual-scientific society interact on an ordinary everyday basis; this example, although very mundane, is nonetheless indicative of what spiritual science requires of us.

In our efforts to find the right perspective on what we have spoken about aphoristically so many times in the past few days, the main thing we have to keep in mind is that the structure and organization of the world as a whole consists of expressions and revelations of real spiritual entities. They are present behind the revealed world, which conceals them from our perception. As you know from many previous lectures, these beings are constantly in movement, constantly inwardly active. At the moment, I am not talking about any particular movement, but about their inner activity as a whole. We have to imagine a certain degree of complexity in this movement if we want to understand how the beings that stand behind certain phenomena relate to the phenomena themselves. The following example will be familiar to you from previous anthroposophical lectures.

We know that our physical evolution began during the Ancient Saturn period and that it continued during the Sun period, when etheric development set in, and so on. But what does our physical development on Ancient Saturn mean in relation to the structure of the cosmos as a whole? It would be totally inaccurate to take our physical nature as it is now and assume that if we imagine it in a much more primitive and simplified form that is what the physical human being would have looked like during the Saturn stage. Nothing could be further from the truth. Perhaps it will help you understand this if I tell you that there is absolutely nothing in the present-day physical world, nothing on the physical plane as it exists now, that bears the slightest resemblance to human physical existence during the Saturn stage of evolution. In none of the forms and facts of the physical world as we know it now is there any trace of what human physical development was like during that evolutionary period. So if we want to understand this ancient form of our physical existence, we must make the effort to do so with a soul and spirit freed from the physical and etheric bodies.

I will call the world in which we understand the make-up of our earliest potential for physical existence during the Saturn stage [writes on the blackboard] the world of the perception of physical human nature on Saturn. For the time being, let me just say that we must leave the physical body and undergo a higher form of development in order to achieve an under-standing of structures corresponding to physical human nature during the Saturn stage.

Next, let us consider human physical existence during the Sun period, which represents a progression of physical evo-lution from the Saturn stage. It is impossible to understand our physical Sun nature with our present-day physical organs of perception. Once again, we must ascend into the spiritual world, but not as high as the level required for compre-hending human physical nature during the Saturn period. In other words, we are able to investigate our physical Sun nature at a somewhat lower level. We can call this [writes on the board] the world of the perception of physical human nature on the Sun.

For investigating physical human nature as it evolved during the Moon period, a still less elevated level of perception is required. As soon as we become capable of body-free perception, we are able to comprehend everything that corresponds to our physical Moon nature. Let us call this third stage in the relationship of the human being to objective fact [writes on the board] the world of the perception of physical human nature on the Moon.

Continuing in the same vein, we come to our physical nature during the Earth stage of evolution. In order to understand this, we do not even need to leave the physical body; we can grasp it with our physical organs of perception. This level of cognition is the natural one for human beings during life on Earth, and we can call it [writes on the board] the world of the perception of physical human nature on Earth.

So, my friends, we have looked at four different levels of the worlds of perception, levels that can also be called [writes on the hoard] physical plane, soul world or astral plane, spirit world or Devachan plane, and higher spirit world or higher Devachan plane.

Higher spirit world, higher Devachan plane	World of perception of physical human nature on Saturn
Spirit world, Devachan plane	World of perception of physical human nature on Sun
Soul world, astral plane	World of perception of physical human nature on Moon
Physical plane	World of perception of physical human nature on Earth

If you follow what I have been describing, you will know that we have to place the physical human being of the Saturn stage here, the physical Sun human here, the Moon human here, and the earthly physical human being here [small circles]. This in no way contradicts our usual concepts, but is indicated quite clearly in my book *An Outline of Occult Science*, where I described at length how what we recognize as human physical nature at the Moon stage is not to be observed on the physical plane, but at a higher level, and so forth.[55] It is all explained there very clearly.

Today we know that human beings have descended during the course of their physical evolution [line connecting the small circles]. The human being, to the extent that we are speaking of our present-day physical nature, is a descending spiritual being. This is one of the basic ancient principles of any spiritual science. Thus, when considering our physical body, we must realize that everything we can see of it at this earth stage in evolution is that aspect of ourselves that has descended the furthest.

However, there is also something concealed in the physical body. It conceals something that is actually Moon-like in nature, something more hidden that is Sun-like in nature, and something still more deeply hidden that is Saturn-like in nature. Thus, within the revealed physical body, the inner character and inner essence are concealed. In a sense, we can actually perceive only a quarter of our physical body. The other three quarters are concealed behind the perceptible body and are nobler and more spiritual in nature than the aspect visible on the physical plane.

Looking at any part of our physical body as it exists now on the physical plane, we have to realize that all our physical organs are in constant inner movement; they are constantly descending and evolving from the spiritual towards the physical. We must understand that as they are growing and developing into their proper form on the physical plane all our organs are involved in a descending course of evolution. They are in the process of evolving downward from a more spiritual form of existence to a more material one.

In assessing the nature and character of anything belonging to a human being, we must be guided by the rule of always finding the right point of view. We are led to the right perspective when we realize that from a certain point of view—the one I have been discussing today—physical human nature is in a process of descent. Therefore, when we look at human development from childhood to maturity, the childhood stage of evolution must be regarded as more spiritual and the mature stage as more material, since a descent from the spiritual to the material has taken place in between. We will not understand human physical development if we look at it from any other point of view. It is only possible to understand it if we are aware that a descent of the physical human being takes place during growth and development, that a growing human being allows something spiritual to descend deeper into matter.

The same principle applies to the world as a whole. Thus, we also speak of cultural evolution. For instance, once upon a time there was an ancient Indian cultural epoch that evolved into the ancient Persian epoch, then into the Egypto-Chaldaean-Babylonian epoch, then into the Graeco-Latin epoch, and finally into our own cultural epoch. However, we also know that former cultural epochs continue to exist alongside more recent ones. 1 have showed you how this manifests in language.

Applied to the human being, this can show us how physical

organs that have proceeded further along the course of descent can exist side by side with others that are still at earlier stages. We will gradually come to see that according to this principle we can distinguish two systems of organs within the human being, although for today I will only point this out aphoristically.

Let us first consider our senses and all the organs that allow us to have sensory perceptions. In terms of their physical structure, these sense organs are all at a certain level; the spiritual has streamed downward to a certain level in these organs. I will make you a diagram of that [sketches on the board]. Now, we said that human nature in its entirety consists of a downward flow; it is moving in this direction [arrow]. The upper horizontal mark indicates the position of the senses within this downward flow, so we must think of all the organs of sensory perception as being at level A.

Next, let us look at a different system of organs, for instance the respiratory system. In order to consider this, too, from the right point of view, we must find the level to which it has descended. Now we will find that the respiratory system stopped at level B. While our sensory system descended to

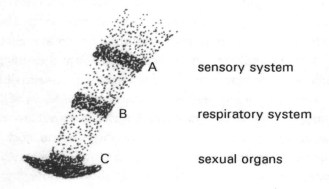

A   sensory system

B   respiratory system

C   sexual organs

level A, our respiratory system continued to descend until it reached level B.

As you might imagine, this process of descent can go on still further, so there could even be a system of organs that has descended still further, to level C. And in fact, our sexual organs have done just that.

There came a time when our physical evolution reached its lowest point and a gradual re-ascent began. However, we will not be able to talk about that today. I will indicate the lowest point of descent with this curved shape at the bottom of the diagram. This is where the earthly process of descent stopped. You can tell from all this that our sensory organs are much more spiritualized than our respiratory organs and everything else. And, as we will come to understand ever more clearly, our sexual organs represent the lowest level of descent. Therefore, all other components of our physical human nature are more spiritual than that particular system of organs.

Now you might say, that was easy enough to understand. That may well be. However, the point I want to make is that psychoanalytic theory, that disgusting philosophy, has been incapable of becoming aware of this simple fact. Psycho-analysts claim that all of people's actions, including mystical experiences, are nothing more than transformed sexual energies. Psychoanalysts, or we might even say materialists in general, take sexuality as their starting point and explain all other human phenomena as metamorphoses of sexuality. I have already pointed out how in Freud's theory everything that happens in a person's life is explained in terms of transformed sexuality. For example, that babies suck on dummies is explained as an expression of infantile sexuality, and so forth.

But what is the truth of the matter? In reality, my friends, any other human daily activity is more spiritual than sexual activity, and to arrive at the right perspective on this subject we have to look at things the other way around. Any attempt to explain what people do by dragging in sexuality and eroticism is completely wrong. The right way of looking at things is to explain sexuality as the transformation of higher human activities into their lowest earthly form.

Since I have been forced to mention the ghastly claims of the psychoanalysts because they are an unavoidable phenomenon of our times, let us take a look at one of the worst of them, namely their contention that the loving childhood relationship of a boy to his mother or a girl to her father is actually a sexual relationship. Psychoanalysts claim that a girl's feelings for her father and a boy's for his mother are sexual feelings, and that boys always view their father as a rival and are unconsciously jealous of him; girls, so they say, are similarly jealous of their mother. This is one of the most terrible of the distortions psychoanalysts have perpetrated. In their writings, as you know, they have even used this assumption as the basis for explaining certain literary works such as the story of Oedipus.

In looking for the right perspective on this subject, we need to ask how adult sexuality develops. As we have seen, it comes about through something spiritual sinking down into matter. Our adult sexuality comes about through the descent of something that was spiritual when we were children. The correct approach is to avoid getting anything not specifically sexual mixed up with sexuality, either consciously or unconsciously, and to realize that sexuality is not yet present in children. Only when we are fully aware of all the ramifications of this can we find the right perspective on the matter.

This is an extremely important point with regard to the education of children, because all kinds of things can go wrong if childish mischief is automatically interpreted as premature sexuality. All kinds of things other than sexuality can be the reason for children misbehaving. Claiming that there is already a sexual side to a child's character is just about the same as insisting that tomorrow's rainy weather is already inherent in today.

By now you will have realized what we are dealing with here—the perspective that has been applied is totally upside down and backward. Coming to such a distorted perspective does not happen naturally, but only by forcing the issue and arbitrarily dragging in our instincts. The whole psycho-analytic approach is tinged with the lowest human instincts; it turns the world upside down. Such an interpretation of the mother-daughter or father-son relationship can only come about if the researcher's subjective instincts get mixed up with the objective course of the study. The consequence of this is, if we follow it to its logical conclusion, that it is per-mitted to apply designations and expressions usually reserved for subjective human actions without at the same time abandoning one's objective standpoint. It would be foolish to apply subjective designations and expressions in objective science. Just imagine someone believes that the hands of a clock are turned by little demons sitting inside— we would call that foolish, of course. Clocks are mechanical devices; there are no little devils inside. Reacting to it objectively, however, we would never say that the person who attributes the clock's functioning to demons is insulting the clock. But when psychoanalysts attribute this sort of sexuality to children, instinctual subjectivity invades their theory. Then it is justified to use subjective expressions and say that the psychoanalytic theory insults human nature. We must make an effort to be truthful and call a spade a spade. In our materialistic world, a number of people have made it their task to cultivate a theory that demeans not only individuals, but human nature in general, to the extent that their whole scientific theory is nothing more than a compilation of insults. When a sufficient number of people realize that this is happening, we will start to see psychoanalytic theory for exactly what it is worth. Then we won't be merely peddling with words any more, but will be able to see things as they are. That's how we can come to clarity on this issue.

Only after we have completely understood everything we have discussed today can our understanding be allowed to consolidate into an insult. When we call psychoanalysis a smutty theory, that is indeed an insult; however, our insight into the objective fact of the matter is what compels us to call it by this name. After all, it would not be right for the criticism to come from the same kind of subjective instincts as the theory itself.

The unique thing about spiritual science, however, is that an apparently abstract theory is transformed into justified feelings and reactions. Those who have gone through a real struggle to understand what psychoanalysis actually is can freely call it a smutty theory without losing their objectivity. It is as objective to call psychoanalysis a smutty theory as it is to say that canvas is white and charcoal black. It is objective terminology derived from true insight into human nature in its totality.

The purpose of our spiritual-scientific view of the world is to deepen our concepts, and not only our concepts but our whole character, my friends. If we say that a society intended as the vehicle for this world-view must be a living organism, then we must also be able to see how the emotions expressed within the context of the society also develop out of this spiritual-scientific world-view, so that even a radical expression such as 'smutty theory' can only be applied when it is firmly rooted in spiritual science and when no personal instincts play a part in its use.

I am sure we will soon find an opportunity for further discussion of related matters.

3.6

How can we work practically on transforming these 'fallen' impulses? Rudolf Steiner did not discuss the role of the lower chakras specifically, but in Knowledge of the Higher Worlds/ How to Know Higher Worlds[56] *he does refer to the 'six-petalled lotus flower' or 'sacral' chakra. This is generally considered to be the one behind people's loves and desires in relationships, (the base one being more to do with physical reproduction, and family or tribe). It is followed by a beautiful imagination from the Grail mysteries, which although from a former age can be helpful in steering us towards a future stage of evolution. The lance or 'magic wand' is perhaps an image of the kundalini[57] rightly used.*

3.6.1 The development of the six-petalled lotus flower

The development of the six-petalled lotus flower, located in the centre of the body, is more difficult still. Its formation requires that we strive for the complete mastery of our whole being through becoming conscious of our self in such a way that, within this consciousness, body, soul and spirit are in perfect harmony. Physical activity, the inclinations and passions of the soul, and the thoughts and ideas of the spirit must be brought into perfect accord with each other. We should purify and ennoble the body to such an extent that our physical organs no longer compel us to do anything that is not in the service of our soul and spirit. The body should not urge upon our soul desires and passions that contradict pure and noble thinking. Nor should the spirit rule the soul with compulsory duties and laws like a slave driver. Rather, the soul should follow these obligations and laws of its own free inclination. As students we should not think of duties as something imposed upon us that we grudgingly perform; we should perform them because we love them.

This means that the soul must become free, poised in perfect balance between the senses and the spirit. We must reach the point in our development where we can surrender to our sense nature because it has been so purified that it no longer has the power to drag us down. We should no longer need to restrain our passions because these follow the right course on their own. Indeed, as long as we still need to mortify ourselves, we cannot advance beyond a certain level of esoteric training. Virtues that we have to force upon ourselves are without value.

As long as we still have cravings, these will interfere with our training even when we try not to give in to them. It makes no difference whether the desires arise from the body or the soul. For example, if we abstain from a certain stimulant in order to purify ourselves by denying ourselves the pleasure it affords, this will help us only if the body does not suffer any discomforts in the process. For the discomfort we experience only indicates that the body still craves the stimulant—and therefore abstention is useless. In such cases, we may have to renounce our aspirations for the time being and wait for more favourable physical conditions—perhaps in a later life. In certain situations, a sensible renunciation is a much greater accomplishment than the continued striving for something that cannot be achieved under existing conditions. Such sensible renunciation advances our development more than the opposite course of persisting despite indications to the contrary.

The development of the six-petalled lotus flower brings us into relation with beings of the higher worlds, but only with those whose existence is also revealed in the soul world. In esoteric training, the development of this lotus flower is recommended only after we have advanced to the point where we can lift our spirit into a still higher world.

3.6.2 The Holy Grail as purifying force

Let us take a look at those very early [initiate] schools. What kind of secret was taught in them? It is only the form of the teaching that changes with time.

The first thing pupils had to understand was that all power of bringing forth that lies outside the animal and human realms may also be seen in the plant world. In spring, the divine power of creation sprouts forth from Mother Earth. It had to be understood that there is a connection between the power that comes forth when the earth covers itself with a green carpet and the power of divine creation. The pupils would be told: 'Out there you see a power in the flowers as they open that concentrates in the seed. Countless seeds will come from the chalice of the flower, and put in the soil they will bring forth something new. One can now feel with the whole of one's being that the events that happen out there in nature are nothing else but the processes that also happen in the human and animal worlds, but in the plant this happens without desire and is wholly chaste.'

The infinite innocence and chastity slumbering in the flower chalices of plants had to live in the hearts of the pupils. They were then told: 'The sunbeam opens the flowers. It brings forth the power from those flowers. Two things come together—the opening flower and the sunbeam. Other realms—the animal and human worlds—are between the plant world and the divine realm. All these realms are only the transition from the plant world to the divine realm. In the divine realm we see once again a realm of innocence and chastity, as in the plant world. In the animal and human worlds we see a realm of desire.'

And then the teachers would speak of the future: 'The time will come when all lusts and desires shall vanish. Then the chalice will open from up above, just as the chalice of a flower opens, and it will look down on the human being. Just as the sunbeam enters into the plant, so will the human being's own purified power unite with this divine chalice.'

We can invert the flower chalice in our minds, letting it bend down from above, from heaven, and we can invert the sunbeam, so that it rises from the human being to the heavens. This inverted flower chalice was shown to be a reality in the mysteries and called the Holy Grail. The real chalice of a plant is the inverted Holy Grail. Everyone who gains esoteric knowledge comes to know that the sunbeam represents something known as the 'magic wand'. The magic wand is a superstitious version of a symbol that represents a spiritual reality. In the mysteries this magic wand was known as the bloodstained lance. We are shown the origin of the Grail on the one hand and of the bloodstained lance on the other, the original magic wand known to true esotericists.

4. Love

4.1

From death—resurrection. Here we consider love in a wider sense, its purpose and mission. Rudolf Steiner did not address marriage in contemporary life specifically as far as I know, except to place it as one of the seven sacraments of the Christian Community. But he did not apparently see it as indissoluble. On the subject of divorce he is understood to have said in conversation that an unhappy couple can part without damage to the children when they reach 18. If this is because of the 'hardness of our hearts' then Love and its Meaning in the World *sets the tone and is so significant that it appears here in entirety. Four further extracts stress additional aspects of love.*

4.1.1 Love and its meaning in the world

When we say that at this point in human evolution people must come to understand the Christ-impulse, we may ask: what, then, is the situation for those who have never heard of the Christ-impulse and may have never even heard the name of Christ? Will such people be deprived of the Christ-impulse because they have not heard the name of Christ? Is it necessary to have some theoretical knowledge of the Christ-impulse for Christ's power to flow into the soul? We will become clear about these questions by the following thoughts concerning human life from birth until death.

Human beings come into the world and live through early childhood half asleep. Gradually, they must learn to experience themselves as 'I'—to find their bearings as 'I' beings and enrich their soul life constantly by what is received through the 'I'. By the time death approaches, this soul life is richest and ripest. Hence, the vital question: what about our soul life after the body falls away? It is peculiar to our physical and soul life that the wealth of our experience and knowledge increases in significance the nearer we approach death; but at the same time certain attributes are lost and replaced by others of an entirely different character.

During our youth we gather knowledge, pass through experiences, cherish hopes that, as a rule, can only later be fulfilled. As we grow older, we begin more and more to love the wisdom revealed by life. Love of wisdom is not egoistic, for this love increases as we approach death. As our expectation of gaining something through wisdom decreases, wisdom increases—our love for this content of soul steadily increases. In this sense, spiritual science may in fact become a source of temptation to the degree that a person may come to believe that the next life will depend on acquiring wisdom in the present one. The effect of spiritual science may be an extension of egoism beyond the bounds of the present life, and this is the danger. Consequently, when understood in the wrong way, spiritual science may become a tempter; this is there in its very nature.

Love of wisdom acquired from life may be compared to the flowering of a plant at the proper stage of maturity. Love arises for something within ourselves. Human beings have often tried to sublimate the impulse of love for something within themselves. We find evidence, for example, of mystics who attempted to transform the urge towards self-love into the love of wisdom, and to let this love shine out in beauty. By immersing themselves through contemplation in the depths of their own soul life, they worked for awareness of the divine spark within themselves. The truth, however, is that the wisdom one acquires in life is merely the means to unfold the seed of the next life. When a plant has completed its growth through the year, the seed remains, and this is also true of the wisdom acquired from life. A human being passes through the gate of death, and the ripening process of the spiritual core of its being is the seed of the next life. Those who feel this may become mystics and mistake what is only the seed of the next life for the divine spark or the Absolute. This is their interpretation, because it goes against the grain for human beings to acknowledge that this spirit seed is simply their own self. Because they knew nothing of reincarnation, Meister Eckhart, John Tauler,[58] and others spoke of it as the 'God within'. When we understand the significance of the law of reincarnation, we recognize the purpose of love in the world, both in a particular and in a general sense. When we speak of karma, we mean the cause in the one life that affects the next. Nevertheless, we cannot truly speak of love in terms of 'cause and effect'. We cannot speak of an act of love and its eventual compensation. True, if there is an action, there will be compensation, but this has nothing to do with love itself. Acts of love do not look for compensation in the next life.

Imagine, for example, that we work, and this leads to gain. It may also happen that our work gives us no joy, since we do it merely to pay our debts, not for actual reward. We can imagine that in this way we have already spent what we are now earning through our work. We would prefer to have no debts, but as things stand we are obliged to work in order to pay them. Now let us apply this example to our actions in general. By everything we do out of love we pay off debts. From an esoteric point of view, what is done out of love brings no payment but is compensation for profit already expended. The only actions from which we have nothing in the future are those we perform out of true, genuine love. This truth may well be disquieting and human beings are lucky in that they know nothing of it in their upper consciousness. But in their subconscious all of them know it, and that is why acts of love are done so unwillingly, why there is so little love in the world. Human beings feel instinctively that they may expect nothing for their 'I' in the future from acts of love. An advanced stage of development must be reached before the soul can experience joy in performing acts of love from which there is nothing to be gained for itself. The impulse for this is not strong in humankind. But esotericism can be a source of powerful incentives for acts of love.

Our egoism gains nothing from acts of love, but the world gains all the more. Esotericism tells us that love is to the world what the sun is for outer life. No soul could thrive if love departed from the world. Love is the 'moral' sun of the world. Would it not be absurd if a person who delights in the flowers growing in a meadow were to wish that the sun would vanish from the world? Translated into terms of the moral life, this means that our deep concern must be that an impulse for sound, healthy development shall find its way into human affairs. To disseminate love over the earth in the greatest measure possible, to promote love on the earth—that and that alone is wisdom.

What do we learn from spiritual science? We learn about the evolution of the earth, we hear of the spirit of the earth, the earth's surface and its changing conditions, the development of the human body, and so on. We come to understand the nature of the forces working and weaving in the evolutionary process. What does this mean? What does it mean when people do not want to know anything about spiritual science? It means that they have no interest in reality. For one can know nothing about the earth if there is no desire to know anything about the nature of Old Saturn, Old Sun, and Old Moon. Lack of interest in the world is egoism in its grossest form. Interest in all existence is humanity's duty. Let us therefore long for and love the sun with its creative power, its love for the well-being of the earth and the souls of human beings. This interest in the earth's evolution should be the spiritual seed of love for the world. A spiritual science without love would be a danger to humankind. But love should not be a matter for preaching; love must and indeed will come into the world through the spreading of knowledge of spiritual truths. Acts of love and spiritual science should be inseparably united.

Love mediated by the senses is the wellspring of creative power, of what is coming into being. Without sense-born love, nothing material would exist in the world; without spiritual love, nothing spiritual can arise in evolution. When we practise love, cultivate love, creative forces pour into the world. Can the intellect be expected to offer reasons for this? The creative forces poured into the world before we ourselves and our intellect came into being. True, as egoists, we can deprive the future of creative forces; but we cannot obliterate the acts of love and the creative forces of the past. We owe our existence to acts of love done in the past. The strength with which we have been endowed by these acts of love is the measure of our deep debt to the past, and whatever love we may at any time be able to bring forth is payment of debts owed for our existence. In the light of this knowledge we will be able to understand the actions of those who have reached a high stage of development, for they have still greater debts to pay to the past. They pay their debts through acts of love, and herein lies their wisdom. The higher the stage of development reached by human beings, the more the impulse of love in them increases in strength; wisdom alone does not suffice.

Let us think of the meaning and effect of love in the world in the following way. Love is always a reminder of debts owed to life in the past, and because we gain nothing for the future by paying off these debts no profit for ourselves accrues from our acts of love. We have to leave our acts of love behind in the world; but they are then a spiritual factor in the flow of world events. It is not through our acts of love but through acts of a different character that we perfect ourselves; yet the world is richer for our acts of love. Love is the creative force in the world.

Besides love there are two other powers in the world. How do they compare with love? One is strength, might; the other is wisdom. In regard to strength or might we can speak of degrees: weaker, stronger or absolute might—omnipotence. The same applies to wisdom, for there are stages on the path to omniscience. It will not do to speak in the same way of degrees of love. What is universal love, love for all beings? In the case of love we cannot speak of enhancement as we can speak of enhancement of knowledge into omniscience or of might into omnipotence, by virtue of which we attain greater perfection of our own being. Love for a few or for many beings has nothing to do with our own perfecting. Love for everything that lives cannot be compared with omnipotence; the concept of magnitude, or of enhancement, cannot rightly be applied to love. Can the attribute of omnipotence be ascribed to the divine being who lives and weaves through the world? Preconceptions born of feeling must here be silent: were God omnipotent, he would be responsible for everything that happens and there could be no human freedom. If human beings can be free, then certainly there can be no divine omnipotence.

Is the Godhead omniscient? Since our highest goal is likeness to God, our striving must be in the direction of omniscience. Is omniscience, then, the supreme treasure? If it is, a vast chasm must forever yawn between human beings and God. If the Godhead possessed the supreme treasure of omniscience for itself and withheld it from us, we would have to be aware of that chasm at every moment. The all-encompassing attribute of the Godhead is not omnipotence, nor is it omniscience—it is love, the attribute that cannot be enhanced. God is uttermost love, unalloyed love, is born as it were out of love, is the very substance and essence of love. God is pure love, not supreme wisdom, not supreme might. God has retained love for himself but has shared wisdom and might with Lucifer and Ahriman. He has shared wisdom with Lucifer and might with Ahriman so that human beings may become free, so that under the influence of wisdom they may make progress.

If we try to find the source of anything creative, we arrive at love; love is the ground, the foundation, of everything alive. It is a different impulse in evolution that leads beings to greater wisdom and power. We make progress through wisdom and strength. When we study the course of human evolution, we see how the development of wisdom and strength is subject to change—there is evolutionary progress, and then the Christ-impulse poured once into humankind through the Mystery of Golgotha. Love did not come into the world by degrees; it flowed into humanity as a gift of the Godhead, completely and perfectly whole. Nevertheless, we can receive that impulse into ourselves gradually. The divine impulse of love as we need it in earthly life is an impulse that came once and forever.

True love is incapable of reduction or amplification. It is very different from wisdom and power. Love does not awaken expectations of the future; it is payment of past debts. Such was the Mystery of Golgotha in world evolution. Did the Godhead, then, owe any debt to humanity?

Lucifer's influence introduced a certain element into human beings; the result was to remove something we had possessed previously. This new element led to a descent; the Mystery of Golgotha countered that and made possible the payment of all debts. The impulse of Golgotha was not intended to remove the sins we have committed in evolution, but to counterbalance what crept into humanity through Lucifer.

Imagine that there are people who know nothing of the name of Jesus Christ, nothing of what is communicated in the Gospels, but who understand the radical difference between the nature of wisdom and might and the nature of love. Such people, even though they know nothing of the Mystery of Golgotha, are Christians in the truest sense. A person who knows that love is there to pay debts and brings no profit for the future is a true Christian. To understand the nature of love—that is to be a Christian. Theosophy, or spiritual science, alone, with its teachings of karma and reincarnation, can make us into great egoists unless the impulse of love, the Christ-impulse, is added; only in this way can we acquire the power to overcome the egoism that may be generated by spiritual science. The balance is established by an understanding of the Christ-impulse. Spiritual science is given to the world today because it is a necessity for humankind, but it contains the great danger that, if it is cultivated without the Christ-impulse, without the impulse of love, human beings will only increase their egoism, will actually breed egoism that lasts even beyond death. We must not conclude from this that we should not cultivate spiritual science; rather we must learn to realize that understanding of the essential nature of love is an integral part of it.

What occurred with the Mystery of Golgotha? Jesus of Nazareth was born, lived as related in the Gospels, and when he was 30 years old he was baptized in the Jordan. Thereafter the Christ lived for three years in the body of Jesus of Nazareth and fulfilled the Mystery of Golgotha. Many believe that the Mystery of Golgotha should be considered entirely from the human aspect, since they view it as an earthly act, belonging to the realm of earth. But that is not true. Only from the vantage point of the higher worlds is it possible to see the Mystery of Golgotha in its true light and how it came to pass on the earth.

Let us think again of the beginning of the evolution of the earth and humankind. Human beings were endowed with certain spiritual powers, and then Lucifer approached them. We can say that at this point the gods who further the progress of evolution surrendered their omnipotence to Lucifer so that humankind might become free. But human beings sank into matter more deeply than was intended; they slipped away from the gods of progress, fell more deeply than had been wished. How, then, can the gods of progress draw humankind to themselves again? To understand this we must not look at the earth but beyond it to the gods taking counsel together. It is for the gods that Christ performs the act through which human beings are drawn back to the gods. Lucifer's deed was enacted in the supersensory world; Christ's deed was enacted in the supersensory world and in the physical world. This achievement is beyond the power of any human being. Lucifer's act belongs to the supersensory world. But Christ came down to the earth to perform his act here, and people are the observers at that deed. The Mystery of Golgotha is an action of the gods, a concern of the gods at which humans are the onlookers. The door of heaven opens and an act of the gods shines through. This is the one and only deed on earth that is entirely supersensory. No wonder, therefore, that those who do not believe in the supersensory have no belief in Christ's deed. The act of Christ is a deed of the gods, an act that they themselves enact. Herein lies the glory and the unique significance of the Mystery of Golgotha, and human beings are invited to be its witnesses. Historical evidence is therefore not to be found because humans have seen the event in its external aspect only; but the Gospels were written from vision of the supersensory and are therefore easily disavowed by those who have no feeling for supersensory reality.

The Mystery of Golgotha as an accomplished fact is one of the most sublime of all experiences in the spiritual world. Lucifer's deed belongs to a time when human beings were still aware of their own participation in the supersensory world; Christ's deed was performed in material existence itself—it is both a physical and a spiritual action. We can understand the deed of Lucifer through wisdom; understanding of the Mystery of Golgotha is beyond the reach of wisdom alone. Even if all the wisdom of this world is ours, the deed of Christ may still be beyond our comprehension. Love is essential for any understanding of the Mystery of Golgotha. Only when love streams into wisdom and then again wisdom flows into love will it be possible to grasp the nature and meaning of the Mystery of Golgotha—only when, as they live towards death, human beings unfold love of wisdom. Love united with wisdom—that is what we need when we pass through the gate of death, because without wisdom that is united with love we die in very truth. *Philosophia*, philosophy, is love of wisdom. The ancient wisdom was not philosophy for it was not born through love but through revelation. There is no such thing as philosophy of the East—but wisdom of the East, yes. Philosophy as love of wisdom came into the world with Christ; there we have the entry of wisdom emanating from the impulse of love that came into the world as the Christ-impulse. The impulse of love must now be applied to wisdom itself.

The ancient wisdom, acquired by the seer through revelation, is expressed in the sublime words from the original prayer of humankind: *Ex Deo Nascimur*, out of God we are born. That is ancient wisdom. Christ, who came forth from the realms of spirit, has united wisdom with love, and this love will overcome egoism. Such is its aim. But it must be offered independently and freely from one being to the other. Hence the beginning of the era of love coincided with the beginning of the era of egoism. The cosmos has its source and origin in love; egoism was the natural and inevitable offshoot of love. Yet with time the Christ-impulse, the impulse of love, will overcome the element of separation that has crept into the world, and the human being can gradually become a participant in this force of love. In monumental words of Christ we feel love pouring into the hearts of human beings: 'Where two or three are gathered together in my name, there am I in the midst of them.'

In like manner the ancient Rosicrucian saying resounds into the love that is wedded with wisdom: *In Christo Morimur*, in Christ we die.

Through Jehovah, human beings were predestined for a group-soul existence; love was to penetrate into them gradually through blood-relationship. It is through Lucifer that the human being lives as a personality. Originally, therefore, human beings were in a state of union, then of separateness as a consequence of the luciferic principle that promotes selfishness, independence. Together with self-ishness, evil came into the world. It had to be so, because without the evil, human beings could not lay hold of the good. When human beings gain victory over themselves, the unfolding of love is possible. Christ brought the impulse for this victory to humans in the clutches of increasing egoism, and thereby the power to conquer evil. The acts of Christ bring together again the human beings who were separated through egoism and selfishness. The words of Christ concerning acts of love are true in the very deepest sense: 'Inasmuch as you have done it to one of the least of these my brethren, you have done it to me.'

The divine act of love flowed back upon the earth; as time goes on, in spite of the forces of physical decay and death, the evolution of humankind will be permeated and imbued with new spiritual life through this act—a deed performed not out of egoism, but solely out of the spirit of love. *Per Spiritum Sanctum Reviviscimus*, through the Holy Spirit we live again.

Yet the future of humanity will consist of something besides love. The achievement of spiritual perfection will be for earthly human beings the most worthy goal to aspire to (this is described at the beginning of my second Mystery Drama, *The Soul's Probation*),[59] but none who understand what acts of love truly are will say that their own striving for perfection is selfless. Striving for perfection imparts strength to our being and to our personality.

But our value for the world must be seen to lie wholly in acts of love, not in what is done for the sake of perfecting ourselves. Let us be under no illusion about this. When a person is endeavouring to follow Christ through love of wisdom and dedicates that wisdom to the service of the world, it only takes real effect to the extent it is filled with love.

Wisdom steeped in love, which at once furthers the world and leads the world to Christ—this love of wisdom also excludes the lie. For the lie is the direct opposite of the actual facts, and those who yield themselves lovingly to the facts are incapable of lying. The lie has its roots in egoism—always and without exception. When through love we have found the path to wisdom, we reach wisdom through the increasing power of self-conquest, through selfless love. In this way the human being becomes a free individuality. Evil was the subsoil into which the light of love was able to shine; but it is love that enables us to grasp the meaning and place of evil in the world. The darkness has enabled the light to come into our ken. Only a person who is free in the real sense can become a true Christian.

4.1.2 The necessity of love

A second force that is also to be found in the hidden depths of our being is the force expressed by the word 'love'. Love is not only something linking people together; it is also needed by them as individuals. When someone is incapable of developing the force of love he, too, becomes dried-up and withered in his inner being. We have merely to picture to ourselves someone who is actually so great an egoist that he is unable to love. Even where the case is less extreme, it is sad to see people who find it difficult to love, who pass through an incarnation without engendering in themselves the living warmth that only arises when we can love at least something on earth.

Such people are a distressing sight, as in their dull, prosaic way they go through the world. For love is a living force that stimulates something deep in our being, keeping it awake and alive—an even deeper force than faith. And just as we are cradled in a body of faith, which from another aspect can be called the astral body, so are we cradled also in a body of love or, as we call it in spiritual science, the etheric body, the body of life forces. For the chief forces working in us from the etheric body, out of the depths of our being, are those expressed in a person's capacity for loving at every stage of his existence. If a person could completely empty his being of the force of love—but that indeed is impossible even for the greatest egoist, thanks be to God, for even in egoistical striving there is still some element of love. Even someone who is unable to love anything else can often begin, if he is sufficiently avaricious, to love money, at least substituting for charitable love another love—albeit one arising from egoism. But if, as I was saying, there were no love at all in a person, the bodily component which should be sustained by love-forces would shrivel, and the person, empty of love, would actually perish; he would really meet with physical death.

This shrivelling of the forces of love can also be called a shrivelling of the forces of the etheric body; for the etheric body is the same as the body of love. Thus at the very centre of a human being we have his essential kernel, the ego, surrounded by its sheaths—first the body of faith, and then round it the body of love.

4.1.3 Mental images as the source of love

By no means should it be said that all our actions stem only
from sober deliberations of the intellect. I am not for a
moment suggesting that only actions proceeding from
abstract judgement are human in the best sense of the word.
But as soon as our conduct rises above the satisfying of purely
animal cravings our motives are always penetrated with
thoughts. Actions springing from love, compassion and
patriotism cannot be analysed by cold abstract concepts. It is
said that here the heart, the mood of soul, holds sway. No
doubt. But the heart and the mood of soul do not create the
motives. They presuppose them and let them enter. Compassion enters my heart when a mental picture appears in my
consciousness of someone who arouses my pity. The way to
the heart is through the head. Love is no exception. Whenever love is not merely the expression of the sexual instinct, it
is based on our mental pictures of the loved one. The more
idealistic those mental pictures are, the more blessed is our
love. Here too, thoughts beget feeling. It is said that love
makes us blind to the failings of the loved one. But it is
equally true that love opens our eyes for the good qualities.
Many pass by these qualities without noticing them. Someone perceives them and, just because he does, love awakens
in his heart. What has he done except to form a mental
picture of what hundreds failed to see? Love is not theirs,
because they lack the mental picture.

4.1.4 Love as the connection with the world

The knowledge we acquire at this sixth stage of initiation is
not dry and rational; it forges an intimate connection

between ourselves and the greater world. Those who achieve this knowledge are intimately related to everything in the world in a way that modern human beings know only in the mysterious relationship of love between man and woman, which is based on a secret recognition of the being of the other person. Looking at the macrocosm through such a relationship, you not only understand but also feel connected with all beings, just as lovers feel connected. You have an intimate, loving relationship to each plant and stone, to all the beings of the world. Our love becomes specialized with regard to each being, which then gives us information it ceased to provide when we descended to modern forms of cognition. Animals eat what is good for them and leave what is harmful; they have a sympathetic relationship to some foods and an antipathetic relationship to others. To develop modern cognition, we humans had to relinquish such direct relationships, but in future we will regain them on a higher level. How do modern esotericists know that a plant's flower affects human beings differently than its root? How do they know that the effect of an ordinary root is different from that of a carrot? They know because things speak to them just as they also speak to animals. At lower levels, such intimate relationships are incompatible with rational consciousness, but at the highest levels we will enter into such relationships consciously.

4.2

The earth's mission is to develop love. More remarkable is the idea that human love is food for the gods—even lower forms—for here Steiner does not dismiss sexual love. Luciferic interference brought about the possibility of choice and we can learn to understand the role of evil. But love is often tinged with egotism. It was the shedding of Christ's blood that made possible the overcoming of dependence on blood relationships and egotism in love. Gradual transformation of our desires and personal loves will lead eventually to a higher, more selfless kind.

This leads us on to consider why Rudolf Steiner viewed marriage as a sacrament. It becomes clear from the extract to the would-be priests preparing for the foundation of the Christian Community that as the seven sacraments correspond to our seven 'bodies' (as described for instance in Theosophy*) marriage corresponds to the stage of Spirit Self or Manas—the stage to be reached by humanity in the forthcoming sixth post-Atlantean epoch. This is when men and women will show further signs of becoming more alike. Marriage enables our souls to reach a state of wholeness as referred to in the introduction. At the stage of Spirit Self we grow into becoming united with our higher self. Uniting the male and female elements within us is a preparatory stage for this, hence the institution of marriage or intimate partnership, during which etheric and astral bodies take on some of the qualities of the other. But Steiner was not rigid with his correspondences. In another sequence given to the priests in 1921, marriage appears to correlate with the stage of Spirit-Man—the final perfected human being. Either way, marriage has a very lofty purpose in enabling us to reach the highest levels intended for humanity.*

4.2.1 Love and self-love

Earth evolution represents the cosmos of love, the previous planet the cosmos of wisdom. On the earth love is to develop from the most elementary stage to the loftiest.

Wisdom, though hidden, permeates the foundation of earth existence; consequently we ought not to speak of a person's physical nature as 'lower', for it is in reality the most perfect aspect of his being. To recognize it one only has to look at the wisdom-filled bone structure, such as the upper thigh bone. Here we find the perfect solution to the problem of how the least expenditure of material can be structured to carry the maximum weight, or think of the wonderful forms of heart and brain. The astral body most certainly is not at a higher stage; it is the *bon viveur* that continually attacks the wise form of the heart. The astral body will need long ages to become as perfect and as wise as the physical body, though it will do so in the course of evolution. The physical body has gone through a corresponding development; it has evolved from lack of wisdom and error to wisdom.

Wisdom developed before love; as yet love is far from perfect, but even now it is to be found at all levels of existence, in plant, animal and human beings, from the lowest sexual love to the highest spiritualized love. Untold numbers of beings who have been created by the urge for love are destroyed in the struggle for existence. Where there is love there is conflict. The occurrence of love brings conflict, necessary conflict. But love will overcome the conflict and transform it into harmony.

The characteristic of physical nature is wisdom; the evolution of the earth began when wisdom became permeated by love. As today there is conflict on earth, so there were errors on the previous planet. Peculiar legendary creatures wandered about, mistakes of nature incapable of evolution. Just as love evolves from lack of love, so wisdom evolves from lack of wisdom. Those who attain the goal of Earth evolution will bring love over to the next planet, as wisdom was originally brought over into Earth evolution. Earthly humanity looks up to the gods as bringers of wisdom; the humanity on the next planet will look up to the gods as bringers of love. On earth, wisdom is given to human beings as divine revelation through beings who were humans on the previous planet. Thus, all realms are interlinked. If there were no plants, the air would soon be polluted. Plants give off life-giving oxygen inhaled by human beings and animals, who in turn exhale carbon dioxide that would destroy the air were it not inhaled by the plants. In this respect, the higher depends on the lower for the very breath of life.

This interdependence applies to all stages and kingdoms. Just as humans and animals depend on the world of plants, so do the gods depend upon mortals. Greek mythology expresses this poetically, saying that from the mortals the gods receive nectar and ambrosia, both words meaning love. Love comes into existence through human beings, and love is food for the gods. The love engendered by mortals is breathed in by the gods. This may seem very strange, yet it is a fact more real than, say, electricity. At first love appears as sexual love and evolves to the highest spiritual love, but all love, the highest as well as the lowest, is the breath of gods. It might be said: if this is so then there can be no evil. But it must be remembered that, just as wisdom is born of error, so love can only evolve and reach perfection through conflict. However, love will be guided by the wisdom that is the foundation of the world.

Not all the beings on the previous planet attained the height of wisdom. Some remained behind and are at a level of development between gods and humans.

Though they still need something from human beings, they can no longer clothe themselves in physical bodies. They are designated as luciferic beings, or collectively by the name of their leader, Lucifer. Lucifer's influence on human beings is very different from that of the gods. The gods approach what is noblest in human nature; a human being's lower nature they cannot and must not approach. Only at the end of evolution can wisdom and love be united. The luciferic beings approach a person's lower nature, the undeveloped element of love, they build a bridge between wisdom and love, thus causing a mingling of the two, with the result that what is impersonal becomes entangled with what is personal.

Wisdom was instinctive on the previous planet, as love is instinctive now. On the previous planet, a creative instinct of wisdom ruled, as now a creative instinct of love. Thus, human beings were formerly guided by instinctive wisdom; then it withdrew its guidance, and we became conscious and aware of ourselves as independent beings.

We are told in the story of Paradise: '... and they saw that they were naked.'[60] That means that human beings saw themselves for the first time; previously they had seen only the external world. They had earth consciousness, but no self-consciousness. The latter enabled them to put wisdom into the service of the self. From then onwards there existed not only selfless love for the surrounding world, but also love of self; the former was good, the latter was bad.

Without Lucifer, human self-consciousness would never have become mingled with love. Thinking and wisdom now became servants of the self; a person could choose between good and evil. But love ought to be directed to the self only in order to place it in the service of the world: the rose should adorn itself only to adorn the garden. That must be deeply engraved in the hearts of those who seek higher development. In order to have a feeling for what is good, we must also have a feeling for what is bad. The gods endowed us with enthusiasm for what is higher; but without evil we would have no feeling of self, no free choice of the good, no freedom.

The good could have become reality without Lucifer, but not freedom. In order to choose the good, we must also have the evil before us; it must exist within us as self-love. When the force of self-love has developed and widened to become love of all, evil will be overcome. Evil and freedom stem from the same original source. Lucifer kindled human enthusiasm for the divine. He is the light bearer; the Elohim are the light itself. Lucifer brought light into human beings by kindling in them the light of wisdom, albeit mingled with the black shadow of evil. The wisdom Lucifer brings is shrunken and blemished, but it penetrates into mortals; he brings external science that serves egoism. That is why selflessness in regard to knowledge is demanded of the esoteric student. Lucifer comes from the old planet; his task on this one is comparable to what the leaven of the old dough means for the new bread. Evil is a good removed from its proper place; what was good on the old planet is no longer so when transferred to ours. The absolute good on one planet brings part of itself as evil to a new planet. Evil is a necessary part of evolution.

One ought not to say that the world is imperfect or incomplete because it contains evil; rather it is complete for that very reason. When a painting depicts wonderful figures of light, together with dark devils, the picture would be spoiled if the devils were removed. The world creator needed evil in order that good could evolve. A good is only good if it has stood the test of evil. For love to reach its highest goal, the love of all, it must pass through the love of self. In *Faust*, Goethe rightly causes Mephistopheles to say: 'I am a part of the power that always intends evil, and always creates good.'

4.2.2 *Overcoming dependence on blood relationships and egoism in love*

The outpouring of the spirit—what effect was it able to have? It was able to bring about that love was tied to the blood. In those early times when tribal communities had not yet developed, people loved one another no less than they do today. In fact, they loved one another more, but it was in the way a mother loves her child and the child his mother. Love was therefore more due to nature. Blood felt drawn to blood, and people felt they belonged together because of this. But the people drawn to such blood-based communities progressed further in their development and this meant that their sympathies became more individual. This led to smaller groupings, families and communities, which then became part of larger communities. Individual people were, however, getting more egoistical and self-seeking. The situation thus was the following. On the one hand humanity was getting more selfish, and on the other hand the influence of Christ made people one. On the one hand we have individualization, with the individual progressively more independent, and on the other the unifying nature of the Christian spirit. These two streams must come fully into their own before it will be possible to have a condition on earth where everyone is independent and on the other hand also connected with everyone else, for each will be filled with the 'Christ-spirit', as it is called.

We must clearly understand that all this is connected with the blood, and that originally something came to expression in human blood that brought to light feeling and inner responsiveness. These would come into play within the blood relationship, but they brought about blood-based love. We must also understand that feelings then became more egoistical. Self-seeking came to be increasingly more present in the blood. That is the secret of human evolution, that the blood gained more and more of the quality of self-seeking. This blood which had grown egoistical had to be overcome.

The principle which was excessive egoism in the human blood ran from the wounds of Christ Jesus on the cross in mystic reality; it became an offering. If this blood had not flowed, self-seeking would have grown more and more in human blood as evolution progressed. The cleansing of the blood from self-seeking—this is what the Mystery of Golgotha achieved. By this deed of love, human blood was saved from its self-seeking.

It is impossible to perceive the cosmic significance of the event on Golgotha if one only sees a human being hanging on a cross, bleeding from a wound made by a lance. The profound mystical significance of this event is that vicariously this is the blood which humanity had to lose in order to be redeemed. We shall never understand the Christian spirit if we take these things in a materialistic sense only, knowing only the material event and not also the spiritual principle which lies behind it. This spiritual principle is the regenerative power of the redeemer's blood that flowed on the cross. We shall only understand the further evolution of the human race if we perceive how crucial this fact is, if we realize that the most tremendous and complete change in humanity's spiritual evolution on earth is connected with this fact.

4.2.3 The transformation of desire and transpersonal love

We could kill off our desires. This would make the personality colourless, however. Yet there is something else we can do, and that is to ennoble them. We need not reduce their strength. We can direct them towards higher objects. The personality need lose nothing of its strength then, though it will grow more noble and divine. We need not kill off desires, only transform them into finer and more noble desires. They can then come into their own with the same vehemence. An example. Think of a honky-tonk. Someone who does not go to one need not be an ascetic. He has merely transformed his lower desires into higher ones and so a honky-tonk would simply bore him.

This is an area where theosophy has been most mis-understood by theosophists. There can be no question of killing off the personal element. It needs to be helped to move up to something higher. Everything theosophy is able to give us will be needed for this. It is thus above all a matter of arousing interest in higher things. This does happen. People need not deaden their feelings for this, but direct them towards the higher, divine process of evolution, to the great realities in this world. If we direct our feelings towards these we will lose interest in the brutal side of life, yet our feelings will not be deadened but will grow rich, and the whole of our human nature will catch fire. If someone is fond of some nice roast pork, it is not a matter of getting rid of this feeling for roast pork but of transforming it. Our aim should be to metamorphose our feelings. The feelings which one indivi-dual has for the symphony of a meal are applied to a real symphony by another. If you preach overcoming desires and activity, you are preaching something impersonal. But if you show people the way in which they can direct their desires to things of the spirit, you point them towards things that are transpersonal. And this transpersonal element must be the goal of the theosophical movement.[61]

The science of the spirit is not intended to produce stay-at-homes and eccentrics but people who are active, going out into the world. How do we reach the transpersonal, however? Not by eating into the personal, but by perceiving what is true, great and all-embracing. This is why it is not for nothing that we cultivate an eye for the great scheme of things in theosophy. This helps us to grow beyond trivial things and take things not in an impersonal way but in one that goes beyond being personal.

There is an area where we can use a crossover experiment,[62] as it were, to establish the difference between personal, impersonal and transpersonal. When it comes to love, you may easily think that the feelings which someone has for someone else are impersonal. But this may be a long way off from anything transpersonal. People fall into a strange illusion here. They confuse self-love with love for someone else. Most people think they love someone else but are in fact loving themselves in the other person. Giving oneself up to someone else is merely something to satisfy our own egoism. The individual concerned is not aware of this, but basically it is just a roundabout way of satisfying one's egoism.

We do not exist in isolation but are part of a whole. A finger is lovingly part of the hand and the organism. It would die if it weren't. In the same way a person could never exist without the rest of humanity. The result of this is that people like people.

Love sometimes simply comes from poverty of soul, and poverty of soul always comes from powerful egoism. If someone says he cannot live without another person, his own personality is impoverished, and he is looking for something that will make him more complete. He dresses it all up by saying: I am getting impersonal; I love the other person.

The most beautiful and selfless love shows itself when one does not need the other person and can also do without them. The individual then loves someone not for his own sake but for the sake of that other person. This does of course mean one has to be able to discern the true value of someone, which can only be done by entering deeply into the world. The more of a theosophist you are, the more you will learn to enter into the inner essence of another individual. And you will then be all the more sensitive of his value and not love him for egoistical reasons. If you go through the world like this, you will also see that some people have one kind of egoism, and others another, each living according to the value of his egoism.

What is needed is higher development of the personality. Impersonal love based on weakness will always also involve suffering. Love that is transpersonal is based on strength and perception of the other person. It can be a source of joy and satisfaction. Swinging to and fro between all kinds of different moods in one's love is always a sign that this love is masked egoism and comes from an impoverished personality. This is how we can best see the difference between impersonal and transpersonal—by looking at love.

4.2.4 The seven sacraments

Participant: In the first instance, the Catholics have more sacraments than the Protestants.

Rudolf Steiner: The things that underlie Catholic dogma go back to certain forms of more ancient knowledge. The idea is that the human being goes through seven stages between birth and death. First birth itself, then what is described as reaching maturity, puberty, then what is described as establishing an awareness of one's inward nature round about the age of 20, then the feeling of being not quite in harmony with the world, of lacking in one's humanity, that is the fourth. And then the gradual growth into the spiritual. These things then started to fluctuate a bit but the whole of human life, including the social aspect, was thought of in seven stages, and it was imagined that the human being grows out of the spirit between birth and death. The Catholic Church no longer recognizes pre-existence in modern times. There is only a thought of God and this growing out of the thought of God is represented in seven stages. These seven stages are [each] complemented by seven other forces. Birth is an evolution, reaching maturity is an evolution, and each form of evolution is complemented by a form of involution: birth through baptism, puberty through confirmation. Each sacrament is the inverse of a natural stage of evolution. We could say that Catholic doctrine represents seven stages of evolution which are complemented by seven stages of involution, and those are the seven sacraments. Four of them are earthly, namely baptism, confirmation, Eucharist, confession. These four are as generally human as the physical body, etheric body, astral body and 'I'. If you go higher, you come to Spirit Self, Life Spirit and Spirit Man. Like a light shining in from the spiritual world, the last three sacraments are those with a social aspect: marriage, holy orders, last rites. The incursion of the spiritual world comes to expression in holy orders. These, then, are the seven sacraments, of which the last three are the last rites, holy orders and marriage. The sacraments are simply the inverse processes for natural processes which human beings undergo and the corresponding rites were instituted in accordance with that.

The idea of the seven sacraments is certainly not an arbitrary one. What is arbitrary is to restrict these seven sacraments to two. That happened in a time in which the feeling for the inner numerical constitution of the world had been lost.

4.3 *The nature of matter and the healing medicine of love*

The mysterious relationship between love and light is revealed here. If we think of light as a form of 'energy', Steiner's view of matter as condensed light is not so far from modern physics. Esoterically, to consider light is to meet with Lucifer (Light-bearer), and his influence in the human body. Here comes the important statement that anyone involved in healing needs to bear in mind. Human love has been compromised by Lucifer and illnesses have arisen (other lectures from the same source describe the ahrimanic effect on illnesses). The true medicine to counteract this is therefore love. Healing of all kinds, but especially so-called spiritual or 'magnetic' healing should arise from love.

There is a fundamental essence of our material earth existence out of which all matter only comes into being by a condensing process. And to the question 'What is this fundamental substance of our earth existence?' Spiritual science gives the answer: 'Every substance upon the earth is condensed light.' There is nothing in material existence in any form whatever that is anything but condensed light. When you know the facts there is no need to prove theories such as the vibration hypothesis of the nineteenth century, when it was attempted to represent light by means coarser than light. Light cannot be traced back to anything else in our material existence. Wherever you reach out and touch a substance, there you have condensed, compressed light. All matter is, in its essence, light.

We have now looked at one side of the question from the point of view of spiritual science. We have seen that light is the foundation of all material existence. If we look at the material human body, that also, inasmuch as it consists of matter, is nothing but a substance woven out of light. Inasmuch as the human being is a material being, he is composed of light.

Let us now consider the other question: 'Of what does the soul consist?' If we applied the methods of spiritual-scientific research to the actual basic essence of the soul we would find that everything that manifests on earth as a phenomenon of soul is a modification, is one of the infinite variety of transformations possible, of that which we call love, provided that we genuinely grasp the intrinsic meaning of this word. Every single stirring of the soul, wherever it occurs, is love modified in some way or other. And when the inner and outer are configured into one, as it were, and imprinted into one another, as is the case in the human being, we find that his outer corporeality is woven out of light and that his inner soul is spiritually woven out of love. Indeed, love and light are interwoven in some way in all the phenomena of our earth existence. For a spiritual understanding of these matters the first question to ask is this: 'How are love and light interwoven in any way?'

Love and light are the two elements, the two components, which permeate all earthly existence: love as the soul constituent of earthly being, light as the outer material constituent of earthly being.

However, for these two elements, which otherwise would exist separately throughout the great course of world existence, to become interwoven, a mediating force is needed that will weave light into love. The power that thus weaves light into the element of love must have no special interest in love; it must be interested only in spreading the light as far as possible, in letting the light stream into the element of love. Such a power cannot be an earthly power, for the earth is the cosmos of love. The earth's mission is to weave love into everything. In other words, everything which is connected with earthly existence is connected with love in some way.

This is where the luciferic beings come into play. They remained behind on the moon, the cosmos of wisdom. They have a special interest in weaving light into love. The luciferic beings are at work wherever and whenever our inner soul, which is woven out of love, enters into any kind of relationship with the element of light in any form; and we are, after all, confronted with light in all material existence. When light touches our being in any way whatsoever the luciferic beings appear and the luciferic quality weaves into the element of love. This is how it came about that human beings, over the course of repeated lives, became associated with the luciferic element: Lucifer became interwoven with the element of love; and all that is formed from love has the imprint of Lucifer, which alone can bring us what causes love to be not merely a self-abandonment but permeates it in its innermost being with wisdom. Otherwise, without this wisdom, love would be an impersonal force in us for which we could not be responsible.

But in this way love becomes the essential force of the 'I' where that luciferic element is woven, which otherwise is only to be found outside in matter. Thus it becomes possible for our inner being, which during its earth existence should receive the attribute of love in its fullness, to be permeated as

well by everything that may be described as an activity of
Lucifer, and from this side leads to a penetration of external
matter; so that which is woven out of light is not interwoven
with love alone, but with love that is permeated by Lucifer.
When we take up the luciferic element, we interweave into
the material part of our own body a soul which is, it is true,
woven out of love but into which the luciferic element is
interwoven. It is that love which is permeated with the luciferic element which impregnates matter and is the cause of
illness working out from within. In connection with what we
have already mentioned as being a necessary consequence of
an illness proceeding from a luciferic element, we may say
that the ensuing pain, which as we have seen is a consequence
of the luciferic element, shows us the effect of the working of
the karmic law. So the consequences of an act or a temptation coming from Lucifer are experienced karmically and the
pain itself indicates what should lead to the overcoming of
the consequences in question.

Ought we to help in such a case or not? Ought we in any
way to remove what has pressed in from the luciferic element
with all its consequences working out in pain?

If we remember the answer to our question as to the nature
of the soul, it follows of necessity that we have the right to do
this only if we find the means, in the case of a person who has
the luciferic element in him which caused his illness, to expel
that luciferic element in the right way. What is the remedy
which exerts a stronger action, so that the luciferic element is
driven out? What is it which has been defiled by the luciferic
on our earth? It is love! Hence only by means of love can we
give real help for karma to work out in the right way. Finally
we must see in that element of love, which has been compromised in the soul realm by Lucifer and caused illness, a

force which must be affected by another force. We must pour in love. We must give love because that which flows in through a deed of love will be helpful. This element of love given as medicine is common to all those approaches to healing which involve the healing of the soul to a greater or lesser extent. All methods of psychological healing are connected in some way with the administering of love. Love is the medicine we give to the other. Love must be the essence of it all. And it surely can be! Even when the psychology involved is straightforward, when all we do is to help another person deal with his depressed state of mind, love is involved. All methods of healing, from the simplest to the more involved methods of healing which are often referred to, rather amateurishly, as 'magnetic healing', must arise out of love.

What does the healer in such a case actually communicate to the one needing to be healed? It is, to use an expression of physics, an 'exchange of current'. What lives in the healer, namely, certain processes in his etheric body, relates in a particular way to the one to be healed, creating a kind of polarity. Polarity arises just as it would in a more abstract sense when one kind of electricity, say positive, is produced and the corresponding other, the negative, appears. In this way polarities are created. This is a supreme deed of sacrifice. We are calling forth a process within ourselves that is not only intended to be meaningful to ourselves, for then one would call forth one process only. In this case, however, the process is intended to call forth in the other the polar opposite. This polarity will depend on the contact established between the healer and the person to be healed; when this is produced, when the opposite process is called forth in the other, this is, in the fullest sense of the word, the sacrifice of a power, the transmuted power of love, a deed of love. This is what works in healing: the transmuted power of love. We must be in no doubt therefore that any endeavour to heal must be carried by this power of love, or else it will fail. Nevertheless, processes of love need not necessarily enter our conscious awareness; they may well take place in the subconscious. Even the techniques of healing, as one might regard them— for example the way the hands are applied—are a reflection of a deed of sacrifice. Even in the case of healing processes where the immediate connections are hidden from us, where we cannot observe what is being done, there is a deed of love involved, even if it has taken on the form of mere technique.

We can see that we may very well intervene by means of soul-related healing—for the reason that the soul essentially consists of love; such healing may appear to involve processes which lie at the periphery of human nature, but it is a fact that that which is love in its essence will be enriched by the love it is in need of. Thus on the one side we see how we can help, so that after being caught in the toils of Lucifer the sufferer is able to free himself again. Because love is the fundamental essence of the soul, we may indeed influence the direction of karma.

4.4

Such a significant consideration leads us on to the wider implications of social life. Here we must become aware of the antisocial forces that lurk within us. Human thinking has the tendency of making us feel more detached. Indeed in the modern epoch of the 'consciousness soul' this is particularly marked. Less and less easily can people 'feel into' another person and know his or her thoughts and feelings. (Perhaps this is why so many people are desperate to share their own as publicly as possible.) Only when we are asleep are we mingled together and laid bare in our souls before one another. We are constantly defending our thinking from being lulled to sleep by the other person. In our feeling life we are bound by our sympathies and antipathies. In the will love determines our actions, but here we usually fall prey to self-deception—it is self-love. Unless we learn to practise self-development, social life will continue to suffer. This lecture was given just after the end of the First World War and Steiner develops his ideas on more political and economic questions in the remainder, which would take us too far from our theme for inclusion here. In the second extract we learn how clairvoyant observation reveals something unexpected that is happening within the etheric or life body when people meet. Such awareness can lead to a better understanding of social life.

4.4.1 Social and antisocial instincts

When social problems or social demands are discussed today, what is generally most completely overlooked is the fact that the social problem cannot really be grasped at all in a manner suited to the requirements of our times without a more intimate knowledge of the human being. No matter what social programmes are thought out, no matter what ideal social conditions we may desire to bring about, if the point of departure is not an understanding of the human being as such, if the objective is not in accordance with the more intimate knowledge of the human being, everything will remain fruitless. I have pointed out to you that the social organization of which I have spoken, this threefold social organization that I have been impelled to present as the important demand of our time, is valid for the present age for the reason that it centres attention upon the knowledge of the human being in every single detail. This is a knowledge of the human being in his present nature in this actual point of time within the fifth post-Atlantean epoch. It is from this point of view that I ask you to consider all the explanations that I shall present.

The foremost consideration is the fact that such a social order as is demanded by contemporary conditions cannot be established apart from a conscious knowledge of the requirement that the human being shall be aware of himself in his relationship to what is social.

We may say that, of all forms of knowledge, the knowledge of the human being himself is decidedly the most difficult. Thus, in the ancient mysteries, 'Know thyself' was set up as the loftiest goal for human endeavour. What is especially difficult for the human being today is the realization of all that works within him out of the cosmos, of how much is at work within him. Since the human being has become especially easy-going today precisely in his thinking, in his conceptions, he likes best of all to conceive of himself in the simplest way possible. But the actual truth is that the human being is by no means a simple being. By means of mere arbitrary conceptions nothing whatever can be accomplished concerning this reality, and in social relationships, likewise, the human being is by no means a simple being. Precisely in social relationships he is such a being, we might even say, as he would passionately desire not to be; he would prefer with the utmost intensity to be different from what he is. It may be said that the human being is really extraordinarily fond of himself. This cannot possibly be questioned. The human being is extraordinarily fond of himself and it is this self-love that causes him to transform self-knowledge into a source of illusions. For instance, a person prefers not to admit that he is only a half-way social being and that to the extent of the other half he is antisocial.

Now, a matter-of-fact and positive admission that the human being is at the same time a social and an antisocial being is a fundamental requirement for a social knowledge of humanity. A person may very well say, 'I aspire to become a social being.' Indeed, he must say this, since if he is not a social being he simply cannot live rightly with his fellow human beings. Yet it is characteristic of human nature at the same time to struggle constantly in opposition to what is social, to remain continuously an antisocial being.

We have repeatedly, from the most varied points of view, considered the human being in accordance with the threefold character of his soul, according to thinking, or conceiving, feeling and willing. Today we may also thus consider him in his social relationships from this point of view. Foremost of all, we must see clearly as regards conceiving, thinking, that in this inner activity there is a source of the antisocial in the human being that is tremendously significant. Through the fact that the human being is a thinking being, he is antisocial. In this matter only the science of the spirit has any access to the truth of things because it is only the science of the spirit that can cast light upon the question as to how we stand in general as human beings related to other human beings.

When is the right relationship established, then, from person to person for ordinary everyday consciousness—or—better expressed—for ordinary everyday life? Well, when this right relationship from person to person is established undoubtedly the social order also then exists. But it is a curious fact—we might say unfortunately, but the one who knows says necessarily—that we develop a right relationship from person to person only in sleep. Only when we are asleep do we establish a true and straightforward relationship from person to person. The moment you turn your back on the ordinary day consciousness while you are in the state of dreamless sleep between falling asleep and waking, you are then, with regard to your thinking—and I speak now solely with regard to conceiving and thinking—a social being. The moment you awake, you begin to develop through your conceptual life, through your thinking, antisocial impulses. It is really necessary to realize how complicated human relationships in society become through the fact that a person takes the right relationship towards other people only in sleep. I have indicated this in various ways from other points of view. I have pointed out, for example, that a person can be thoroughly chauvinistic while awake, but that when he is asleep he is placed actually in the midst of those people, is associated with those people, especially with their folk spirit, whom he hates most of all while awake. Nothing can be done about this fact. Sleep is a social leveller. But, since modern science is unwilling to know anything whatever about sleep, it will be a long time before science will accept what I have just said.

We enter through our thinking into still another antisocial stream in the waking state. Suppose you stand face to face with a person. In truth we confront all human beings only through confronting individual persons. You are a thinking human being, naturally, since you would not be human if you were not a thinking being. I am speaking now only about thinking; we shall speak later about feeling and willing. From the point of view of feeling and willing some objection might be raised, but what I am now saying is correct as regards the standpoint of conceiving. When you stand as a conceiving, thinking human being in the presence of another person, it is a strange fact that the reciprocal relationship that comes about from person to person brings into existence in your subconscious the tendency to be put to sleep by the other person. You are actually put to sleep in your subconscious by the other person. This is the normal relationship from person to person. When you come together, the one strives—and, naturally, the relationship is reciprocal—to put to sleep the subconscious of the other. What must you do, therefore, as a thinking person? (Of course, everything that I am telling you takes place in the subconscious. It is a fact even if it does not rise into ordinary consciousness.) Thus, when you come into the presence of a person, he puts you to sleep; that is, he puts your thinking to sleep, not your feeling and willing. Now, if you wish to continue to be a thinking human being, you must defend yourself inwardly against this.

You must activate your thinking. You have to take defensive measures against being put to sleep. Confronting another person always means that we must force ourselves to awake; we must wake up; we must free ourselves from what this person wants to do to us.

Such things actually occur in life, and we actually comprehend life only when we view it in a spiritual-scientific way. If you speak to a person, or even if you are merely in the company of a person, this means that you must continuously keep yourself awake against his endeavour to put you to sleep in your thinking. Of course, this does not come into the ordinary consciousness, but it works within the human being. It works in him as an antisocial impulse. In a certain sense every person confronts us as an enemy of conceptual life, as an enemy of our thinking. We must defend our thinking against the other person. This requires that we are in great measure antisocial beings as regards our conceptual life, our thinking, and can become social beings only by educating ourselves. If we were not compelled constantly to practise such protection, to which we are compelled through the necessity within which we live—if we did not have to practise constantly such protection against the other person, we could be social human beings in our thinking. But, since we must practise this, it is of utmost importance for us to realize perfectly clearly that it is possible for us to become social beings, to become such through self-discipline, but that as thinking human beings we are not actually social to begin with.

From this fact it becomes clear that no assertions whatever can be made regarding the social question without investigating the life of the soul and the fact that the human being is a thinking being because the social question penetrates into extremely intimate matters in human life. Whoever does not take account of the fact that the human being simply develops antisocial impulses when he thinks will arrive at no clarity in regard to the social problem.

During sleep things are easy for us. First of all, we are simply sleeping. There, in other words, bridges can be built connecting all men. In the waking state the other person, as he confronts us, seeks to put us to sleep in order that a bridge may be built to him, and we do the same to him. But we must protect ourselves against this. Otherwise we should simply be deprived of our thinking consciousness in our intercourse with human beings.

Thus it is not so easy to enunciate social demands since most people who set forth social demands do not become at all conscious of the depth to which the antisocial is rooted in human nature. People are least of all inclined to state such things to themselves as self-knowledge. It might become easy for them if they would simply admit, not that they alone are antisocial beings, but that they possess this quality in common with all other people. Even when a person admits that human beings are in general antisocial beings as thinkers, everyone secretly clings to the reservation as regards themselves that they are an exception. Even if they do not state this fully to themselves, there always shines dimly and secretly in their consciousness the thought that they are an exception and the others are antisocial beings as thinkers. The truth is that it becomes exceedingly difficult for people to take seriously the fact that it is not possible as a human being to be something, but it is always necessary as a human being to become something.

People deceive themselves in a terrible way about themselves when they believe they can point to something absolute that determines a sort of special perfection in their case. In the human being everything not in the process of becoming evidences an imperfection. What I have said to you regarding the human being as thinker, and regarding the antisocial impulses produced as a result, has still another important aspect.

The human being alternates in a way between the social and the antisocial, just as he alternates between waking and sleeping. We might even say that sleeping is social and waking is antisocial, and just as the human being must alternate between waking and sleeping in order to live a wholesome life so must he alternate between the social and the antisocial. But it is just this fact that we have to take into account when we reflect about human life. For you see, a person may thus tend more or less towards the one or the other, just as a person may tend more or less towards sleeping or waking. There are persons who sleep beyond the normal amount. In other words, they, in the condition of a swinging pendulum in which the human being must be between sleeping and waking, simply tend towards one side of the scale. In the same way a person may cultivate within himself in greater measure either the social or the antisocial impulses. Human beings are in this respect differentiated individually in that one cultivates more the social and another the anti-social impulses. If we possess a knowledge of human beings in any measure, we can differentiate people in this way.

Now, I said that there is another aspect of this matter. The antisocial in us is connected with the fact that we protect ourselves in a certain way against being put to sleep. But something else is connected with this. It makes us ill. Even if the diseases that arise from this cause are not very evident— although sometimes they are—yet the antisocial nature of the human being belongs among the causes of illness. Thus it will be easily intelligible to you that the social nature of the human being at the same time possesses a healing quality, something that gives life. But you see from all this how extraordinary human nature is. A person cannot heal himself by means of the social elements in his nature without in a certain way putting himself to sleep. As he tears himself away from this social element, he strengthens his thinking con-sciousness, but becomes antisocial. But in this way he also paralyses his healing forces, which are in his subconscious, in his organism. Thus the social and antisocial impulses present in the human being produce their effects even to the extent of determining a sound or an ill constitution of life.

One who develops a knowledge of the human being in this direction will be able to trace a great number of more or less genuine illnesses back to his antisocial nature. The state of illness depends, much more than is supposed, upon the antisocial nature of the human being, especially as regards those illnesses that are often genuine but that manifest themselves outwardly in some such thing as moodiness, in all sorts of self-torment, torment of others, in 'feeling odd' and in the struggle to get through something disagreeable. All such things are connected with an unsound organic constitution, and they gradually develop when a person is strongly inclined towards antisocial impulses. In any case, it ought to be entirely clear that an important mystery of human life is here concealed. This mystery of life, important both for the teacher and also for the human being's self-education if it is known in a living and not merely theoretical way, means that a person acquires the inclination to take his own life strenuously in hand, to think about mastering the antisocial element in order to reach the mastery of it. Many persons would cure themselves not only of their moodiness but also of all kinds of ailments if they would thoroughly investigate their own antisocial impulses. But this must be done in a serious way. This must be done without self-love because it is something of the utmost importance for our lives.

This is what must be said in regard to the social and the antisocial elements in the human being in reference to his conceptual life, or his thinking.

In addition, the human being is a feeling being, and there is something peculiar, in turn, as regards his feelings. In respect to feeling the human being is also not so simple as he would like to think. Feeling between two human beings, in other words, shows a most paradoxical peculiarity. Feeling has the peculiar characteristic of being inclined to give us an untrue sentiment in regard to the other person. The first inclination in the subconscious of a person in interaction between human beings always consists in the fact that an untrue sentiment arises in his subconscious regarding the other person. In our lives we must, first of all, continually oppose this untrue sentiment. One who knows life will easily observe that those people who are not inclined to show an interest in other people are really critical about almost all people—at least after a certain time. This is really a peculiarity of a great many people. They love one person or another for a certain length of time but, when this time has passed, something is aroused in their nature and they begin in some way to be critical of the other, to hold something or other against him. Often the person himself does not know what he has against the other because these things take their course to a large extent in the subconscious. This is due to the fact that the subconscious simply has a tendency actually to falsify the picture that we form of the other person. We must learn to know the other person more deeply, and we shall then see that we must erase falsification in the picture we have acquired of him.

Paradoxical as it may sound, a good maxim to live by, even though there would have to be exceptions, would be to endeavour always to correct in some way the image of the human being that becomes fixed in our subconscious, which has the tendency to judge human beings according to sympathies and antipathies. Even life itself demands this of us. Just as life requires us to be thinking persons and we thus become antisocial, so does life—and what I am telling you is based upon facts—demand that we judge according to sympathies and antipathies. But every judgement based upon sympathies and antipathies is falsified. There is no real judgement that is correct if it is formed according to sympathies and antipathies. Since the subconscious in the feelings is governed by sympathy and antipathy, it always sketches a false picture of the other person. We simply cannot form in our subconscious a true picture of him. To be sure, we often have a picture that is too favourable, but the picture is always formed according to sympathies and antipathies. And there is nothing we can do about it except simply to admit this fact and to admit that, also in this regard, we simply cannot be something as human beings but can only become something. Especially as regards our interaction in feeling with other individuals we must simply lead a 'waiting' life. We must not act in accordance with the image of them that presses upward out of the subconscious into consciousness; but we must endeavour to live with people, and we shall see that the social attitude evolves out of the antisocial attitude that one really always has.

For this reason it is of special importance to study the feeling life of the human being to the extent that it is antisocial. Whereas the thinking life is antisocial because he must protect himself against falling asleep, the feeling life is antisocial because he governs his interaction with other people according to sympathy and antipathy, and from the beginning injects false currents of feeling into society. What comes from people through the influence of sympathies and antipathies is certain from the beginning to interject antisocial currents of life into human society.

Paradoxical as it may sound, we might say that a social community would be possible only if people did not live in sympathies and antipathies, but in that case they would not be human beings. You see clearly from this that the human being is at the same time a social and antisocial being, and that what we call the 'social' question requires that we enter into intimate details of his nature. If we do not do so we shall never attain to a solution of the social question for any period of time whatever.

As regards the volition acting between individuals it is really striking and paradoxical to discover what a complicated being the human being is. You know, of course, that not only sympathies and antipathies play their roles in the relationship between individuals as regards the will—as these do also to the extent that we are feeling beings—but that here inclinations and disinclinations which pass into action also play a role. That is, sympathies and antipathies in action, in their expression, in their manifestation, play a special role. One person behaves in relation to another person according to how he is influenced by his special sympathy towards the person, the special degree of love that he brings to meet the other person. There an unconscious inspiration plays a strange role. For everything that involves all relationships in will between people must be viewed in the light of the impelling force that underlies these volitional relationships, that is, in the light of the love that plays its role in greater or lesser degree. Indeed, individuals cause their will impulses, which are active in this way from one to the other, to be sustained by this love that is active between them.

Regarding the feeling of love, people are subject in pre-eminent degree to a great illusion, which requires a greater measure of correction than the ordinary sympathies and antipathies in their feelings. However strange it may seem to the ordinary consciousness, it is entirely true that the love manifesting itself between one person and another, if it is not spiritualized—and love is actually seldom spiritualized in ordinary life, even though I am not speaking merely of sexual love or love resting upon a sexual foundation, but in general of the love of one person for another—is not really love as such, but an image the person makes of love. It is generally nothing more than a terrible illusion, because the love one person believes he feels towards another is for the most part nothing but self-love. A person supposes that he loves another, but in this love really is loving himself. You see here a source of an antisocial disposition that must be the source also of a terrible self-deception. In other words, a person may suppose that he is giving himself up in an overwhelming love for another person, while he really does not love the other person at all. What he feels as a state of rapture in his own soul in association with the other person, what he experiences within himself by reason of the fact that he is in the presence of the other person, that he makes declarations of love, if you like, to the other person—this is what he really loves. In the whole thing the person loves himself as he kindles this self-love in his social relationship with the other person.

This is an important mystery in human life and it is of enormous importance. This love that a person supposes is real, but that is really only self-love, self-seeking, egoism, masked egoism—and in the great majority of cases the love that plays its role between people and is called love is only masked egoism—is the source of the greatest imaginable and the most widespread antisocial impulses. Through this self-love masked as real love, a person becomes in pre-eminent degree an antisocial being. Indeed, the human being is an antisocial being in that he buries himself within. He buries himself within most of all when he is unaware of it, or wishes to know nothing of it.

Thus you see that the person who speaks about social demands, especially as regards contemporary humanity, must consider fully such soul states. We must simply ask, 'How shall human beings arrive at any social structure in their common life if they will not learn to understand how

212 SEXUALITY, LOVE AND PARTNERSHIP

much self-seeking is embodied in so-called love, in the love of one's neighbour?'

Thus love can actually become an enormously strong force working in the direction of the antisocial life. It may be asserted that a person, when he is not working upon himself, when he does not take himself in hand through self-discipline, is invariably an antisocial being when he loves. Love as such, as it inheres in the nature of the human being, is predestined to be antisocial unless the person is practising self-discipline, for it is exclusive. Once more, this is no criticism. Many of the requirements of life are connected with the fact that love must be exclusive. In the very nature of things, a father will love his own son more than a strange child, but this is antisocial. If people assert, as the habit is nowadays, that the human being is social, this is nonsense; for the human being is just as strongly antisocial as he is social. Life itself makes him antisocial.

4.4.2 *The action of the etheric body in human encounter*

If a person is only capable of observing the meeting of two people with his physical sensory vision, he merely notices that they come together, greet one another, and so on. But when he becomes able to observe such an event spiritually, he will find that each time two human beings meet a spiritual process is established, which among other things is also expressed outwardly in the fact that the part of their etheric bodies which forms the head becomes the expression of every feeling of sympathy and antipathy that the two people feel for each other; and this continues as long as they are together.

Suppose two people were to meet who could not bear each

other—an extreme case, but there are such in life. Suppose two people meet who dislike each other, and that this feeling of antipathy is mutual. It can then be seen that that part of the etheric body which forms the head projects beyond the head in both cases, and that both the etheric heads incline towards each other. A mutual antipathy between people meeting is expressed as a continual bowing and inclination of the etheric head of each towards the other. When two people come together who love each other, a similar process can be observed; but then the etheric head inclines back, it bends backwards. Now whether the etheric head bends forwards as though in greeting when antipathy is felt, or bends backwards where love is felt, in both cases the physical head then becomes freer than it would be otherwise. This is of course always relative; the etheric body does not entirely emerge but extends in length, so that a continuation can be observed. A more rarefied etheric body then fills the physical body than is normally the case, and the result of this, by reason of the exceptional transparency of the etheric body, is that the astral body remaining inside the head becomes more clearly visible to clairvoyant vision. So that not only is there a movement of the etheric body but also an alteration in the astral light of the head.

It is then, my dear friends, no poetic imagination but an actual fact that the reason that in places where such things are understood people who are capable of selfless love are represented with an aura round their heads, which is known as a halo. When two people meet, with simply a strong tinge of egotism in their love, this phenomenon is not so apparent. But if a person relates to humanity at certain times when he is not concerned with himself and his own personal relation to another, but is filled with a universal human love for all humanity, such phenomena appear. At such times the astral body in the vicinity of the head becomes clearly visible. If there are persons then present who are able to see this in a person clairvoyantly, they can see the halo and feel obliged to paint or represent it as a reality. These things are absolutely connected with the objective facts of the spiritual world; but that which is thus objectively present, and which is a lasting reality in the evolution of humanity, is still connected with something else.

4.5 The connection between memory and love and the confusion of love and sexuality

The role of the 'I' and its relevance to love is treated next, also its relation to memory—for example a strong memory of a beloved person who has died has a liberating effect on the 'I'. Rudolf Steiner concludes by reiterating the view that our present age confuses love with sexuality and that this leads to a denial of the true human 'I' or spirit.

Let us now consider the 'I'. In sleep, likewise, the 'I' leaves the physical and etheric bodies behind and unites outside them with cosmic things and processes. Thus we become aware of how, as human beings, we are able to dive down into things with our own actual being—even if the experience remains unconscious. The 'I' itself, at any rate, certainly emerges from deep sleep and enters into the physical and etheric bodies. But only spiritual-scientific initiation can follow this process. As far as our memory of it is concerned, the way the dream force slips into the physical being provides ordinary observation with something to hang onto as we try to understand it. To do this, one must learn to observe with

Imagination when we develop it in the way I have described in *How to Know Higher Worlds*.[63]

Having learned to observe with Imagination, we can learn to observe how the 'I' (which resides with cosmic things and processes during sleep) is submerged in the physical and etheric bodies. We can also learn to observe the transformation undergone by the 'I' when it emerges from the darkness of sleep. To present-day human development on earth, the 'I' at first seems powerless, sunk in the darkness of sleep, in the darkness of the soul. Yet when it plunges into the physical and etheric bodies, it strengthens itself there. It becomes wrapped up in the paths opened by the physical and etheric bodies. It takes hold of the force of the blood, and works through the inner power of blood.

This is shown in waking day consciousness. The 'I', immersing itself in the physical and etheric bodies, manifests itself. The 'I' is what weaves and works as the free element in the human being. It may show itself, or not. And when it does, what is its characteristic manifestation?

When the 'I' manifests, it is the force of love that appears in humanity. We would never have the capacity to open into another being or another process—to pass, as it were, into the other—if the 'I' did not leave us every night to immerse itself in the things and processes of the outer cosmos. It really is submerged there. When the 'I' slips into us in waking consciousness, it communicates within us the ability to love that it attained outside.

This, then, is what rises up in the depths of your inner life as the threefold power of the soul: freedom, the life of memory, and the force of love. Freedom is the etheric body's inner primordial form. Memory is the astral body's dream-forming force arising within us. Love is the guiding force that arises within us so that we can surrender ourselves dedicatedly to the outer world.

When—and to the extent that—the human soul participates in this threefold force, it is transfused with spiritual life. When thoroughly imbued with these three forces—the sensation of freedom, the force of memory (which allows us to connect past and present) and the force of love through which we can give our inner life for the outer world and unite with it—our soul is 'spiritualized'. The inner possession of these three powers permeates the soul with spirit.

To grasp this with the right nuance of soul is to grasp that human beings bear the spirit within their souls. Whoever does not understand the spirit's threefold inner penetration of the soul—through freedom, memory and love—will not understand how the human soul can shelter the spirit.

The consequences of this extend over the whole of life. Something wonderful can definitely be attained once we are able to establish an inner, living connection between memory and love: the power of memory presiding in us by virtue of the astral body, the power of love given by the 'I'.

These things may be directly grasped in life. We preserve the memory of a beloved one who has died beyond death. We carry the person's image in our soul. We combine the sensory impressions that we received when the person was alive with what remains when their sensory existence is taken away from us. We continue to live with the dead in memory with all the power and intensity of our soul to the point that we no longer need the support of external sensations. We try to bring such a living quality to these memories that it may seem as if the dead were there, with us, as if truly living—as if we had a direct apprehension of their 'livingness'. We remain conscious that we bear these things in our memory, but we connect it with the force that came about as the result of the strengthening of the astral body—the force that we received through our 'I', the force of love. We carry this intense love for the dead over and beyond the grave. Previously we were able to develop the force of love under the influence of sensory stimulation. Now we became capable of connecting the force of love with the image that is no longer aroused by the senses.

Thus, it is possible to strengthen what otherwise would only be expressed by the astral body and the 'I' when they made use of the physical organs. This is a way to rise inwardly to a certain level of separation from the astral body and 'I'. You preserve the memory of the dead (which can no longer be stimulated by the physical and etheric bodies) and hold it so intensely and animatedly that you are able to unite it with intense love. One of the first steps towards liberating the 'I' and the astral body from the physical and etheric bodes while awake rests precisely in the memory that we can preserve of the dead.

If we could only understand the significance of keeping memory alive, we would be on the path that leads over the threshold between the physical and spiritual worlds. If we could only understand what it means to contemplate the image that is all that is left of the dead in the same way as we contemplate the living person, we would experience the liberation of the astral body and the 'I'.

We would have the following experience or jolt. At first, we have the living memory, as if the person who died were still there. We know that in our waking consciousness we have connected the image of the dead person with the love that we once used to feel only under the influence of sensory impressions from the then living person. We make all this

active and alive within us. When we can develop the necessary inner strength, then the jolt comes. We step over the
threshold into the spiritual world. The dead person is present
in full reality.

This is one of the paths that human beings can take into the
spiritual world. It is connected with things in the face of
which one can feel only reverence. Even when we understand
them, we can experience them only with reverence and a
certain serious inner gravity.

This is one example of crossing the threshold into the
spiritual world.

We must allow all the seriousness associated with such
ideas to work on our souls. We must make this seriousness
real. Then we will have an idea of the seriousness that must
be united with any crossing into the spiritual world. If we
truly wish to enter the spiritual world—if in all earnestness we
wish to grasp it—life must have shown us its deep seriousness
because we willed it so. The science of initiation has always
attempted to infuse this seriousness into culture and civilization. This is what our externalized age needs again today.

It is a remarkable sign of the times that dogmatic science
means more to people today than reality. A person can
become conscious of his or her freedom in every moral act.
As human beings, we can actually experience freedom just as
we can experience red or white. But we deny our freedom.
We deny it under the authority of contemporary science.
Why? Because contemporary science sees only the mechanical, where what comes earlier is always the cause of what
comes later. Therefore this science states dogmatically that
everything must have a cause. It dogmatically affirms causality. Because causality must be correct, because we swear by
causality as a dogma, we deafen ourselves to the feeling of

freedom. Reality is buried in darkness to protect dogma—in this case the dogma of a powerful science exercising its authority. Science abolishes life. If life became aware of itself in us, this life would directly grasp freedom in the activity of thinking. And so a purely external science building on causality has become the great murderer of the feeling of life of human beings. We must become conscious of this.

Can we then hope that, having inwardly destroyed the experience of freedom, human beings can push forward to the spirit—the spiritual form of memory? Can we hope that, just as they normally allow red to be a revelation of the red rose, human beings will allow memory to reveal to them the force of dream welling up and working in the universe? Can we hope that having killed the feeling of freedom in the first stage by the dogma of so-called causality, human beings will acquire the necessary conviction to rise to the second stage?

Human beings fail to see the spirituality of their own souls. They fail to reach to a level deep enough to see clearly that, besides the ability to live among things in our sleep, we can attain the ability in our spiritual 'I' to love through our spirit. The deepest foundation of love is an 'I' penetrated with spirit that submerges in the physical and etheric organism. To know the spiritual nature of love means in a certain sense to know the spirit. Whoever knows love knows the spirit. But this requires that a person penetrate to the innermost spiritual experience of love in the knowledge and experience of it. Here is where our civilization has taken a wrong turn.

Memory means moving and living in the inner soul. In our inner souls, however, distinctions are not so easily made. Only mystics like Swedenborg, Meister Eckhart and Johannes Tauler[64] could go deep into their inner souls, their memories, and experience the movement and life of the eternal spirit there. They speak of the little spark that lights up in human beings when they become aware within, in memory, that the same thing that lives in the microcosm lives and works outside in the creative, formative forces whose dreaming lies at the foundation of all world existence. This deep inner soul memory, however, is of course difficult to attain. Things are not so clear there.

Things become very clear when we move to the third stage, when we see how at the third level our civilization has mis-understood the original spiritual being and weaving of love. All things spiritual naturally have an outer sensory form, for the spirit submerges in the physical constitution. The spirit incarnates in the physical. If the spirit forgets what it is, if the spirit is only conscious of the physical, it will seem as if the physical activates what is actually activated by the spirit. This is the great delusion of our time.

Our time does not know love. Our age fantasises about love, lies about love. In reality, when it tries to think of love it only knows erotic love. I am not saying that the individual person does not experience love. Human beings are less likely to deny the spirit in their unconscious feelings, in their unconscious will than in their thinking. But whenever the present civilization thinks of love it just says the word. It actually means eroticism. It is fair to say that you should read through all current literature from end to end and whenever the word 'love' appears replace it with the word 'eroticism' or 'sexual love.' For 'sexual love' is all that materialistic thinking knows of love. Denial of the spirit turns the force of love into an erotic force. In many areas, not only has the genius of love been supplanted by its lowly servant eroticism, but also its counter-image, the demon of love, has stepped in. The demon of love appears when something that was at work in human beings as divinely willed is taken over by human thinking and torn from spirituality by intellectuality.

This is how it goes. Recognize the genius of love, and you will have love infused with spirit. Acknowledge love's lowly servant, and you will have eroticism. But we have fallen prey to the demon of love. And the genius of love has its demon in the way that current civilization interprets—not in its real form—in the way it interprets sexuality. Nowadays, in fact, when we wish to speak of love, we no longer even speak of eroticism, but instead only of sexuality!

Such talk about sexuality in our civilization includes much that passes for sexual education. The demon of love lives in all this intellectualized talk about sexuality. The genius of an age always appears in the form of its demon, for the demon steps in wherever the genius is denied. This is equally true of this realm, where the spiritual in its most intimate form, love, should appear. Our age often prays not to the genius of love but to the demon of love, and confuses the true spirituality of love with the demonology of love in sexuality.

Naturally, in this area in particular the most complete misunderstandings occur. For what lives at the core of sexuality is of course saturated by spiritual love. But humanity can fall from this spiritualization of love. And it is most likely to fall in the age of intellectualism. When the intellect takes the form I described yesterday, then what is spiritual in love is forgotten, and only its external form is considered.

It is in the power of human beings to deny their own being. They deny it when they sink down from the genius of love to the demon of sexuality—by which I mean above all the way our present time feels these things, the way they are mostly present.

4.6

The last three extracts deal with ideas of love and karma. The fact that we have had a number of earth lives now makes it harder to relate to others, to really experience them because these memories of earlier lives live in the subconscious and overshadow our relationships. We try to love one another but cannot. Becoming conscious of these karmic hindrances is the first step. But when we can truly act from love, then joy comes back to us in a future incarnation. This in turn will lead to insight into things that are beautiful, good and true. Deeds done from only a sense of duty, however, bear the consequence of indifference coming towards us next time round. How can we learn to understand the whole human being who passes through many lifetimes? Paradoxically perhaps, the answer lies in developing an awareness of how oneself might have been in a former lifetime and learning to love that person as if he or she were someone else—precisely because such a person is a stranger to us. Thus understanding karma and reincarnation is not abstract and neither need it be fanciful. A true relationship to our previous earth lives goes hand-in-hand with overcoming egotistic love and growing towards that state of love which now Christ and the highest beings bear towards ourselves.

4.6.1 The influence of karma on human relationships

The way human beings turn in upon themselves has already become their most salient characteristic, and they will continue to do this more and more. It is the consciousness soul that gives people this characteristic of being shut up in themselves, locked away from the rest of humanity and living in isolation. Hence it is more difficult to get to know other people, let alone achieve real familiarity or intimacy. You have to go through a complicated rigmarole of becoming acquainted before you can get on intimate terms with someone.

What is the purpose of all this? To gain some insight into it let us consider one specific truth from spiritual science which tells us that there is absolutely no question of the way we meet each other today being a matter of mere chance. The paths of our lives bring us together with certain people and not with others. This results from the effects of our individual karma, for we have entered a period of evolution that in some senses has brought to a culmination the earlier karmic developments undergone by human beings. Think how much less karma people had accumulated in earlier periods of earthly evolution. Every time we incarnate, new karma is formed. Initially people had to encounter one another under conditions that did not entail having met before, so the relationships they developed were entirely new. Having meanwhile incarnated on the earth many, many times, we have now reached a stage in which we hardly ever meet someone with whom we have not experienced one thing or another in earlier incarnations. We are brought together with others through what we experienced in earlier incarnations. Although we may appear to meet people by chance, in fact we do so as the result of meeting them in earlier incarnations, when forces were generated that now lead us to meet them again.

The consciousness soul, enclosed within itself as it should become in our time, can only develop if what takes place today between one human being and another is less important than what is now beginning to work, hermit-like, within us—something, namely, that rises up in us as the result of earlier incarnations. When two people met in Graeco-

Roman times they had to make an immediate impression on one another. Now, however, things have to be different so that the more isolated consciousness soul can develop within us. When one person meets another it is what rises up in either of them as the result of earlier incarnations that should begin to work. This takes longer to come about than an instantaneous acquaintance between the two of them based on external appearances. It means that they must allow what they experienced with each other to rise up gradually, in their feelings, in their instincts. This is what is needed today: that in getting to know one another our individualities first have to be pared down. In this kind of getting to know one another through the paring down of individuality, reminiscences and effects of earlier incarnations can rise up, as yet unconsciously and instinctively. The consciousness soul can only form when we enter into relationships with others out of our inner being. The intellectual and mind soul, on the other hand, was formed more through encounters resulting in instantaneous acquaintance.

What I have just described is as yet only in its early stages as far as the fifth post-Atlantean epoch is concerned. As this epoch progresses people will find it more and more difficult to achieve appropriate relationships with one another, for this attainment of appropriate relationships now entails the application of inner development, inner activity. This has already begun, but it will become more and more widespread and intense. Even now it is already difficult for people brought together by karma to understand one another directly. One reason is that other karmic connections may be sapping their strength, so that they lack the energy to bring to the fore instinctively everything they have in them from earlier incarnations.

People are brought together and love one another; certain influences from earlier incarnations bring this about. But then other forces work against this when reminiscences of this kind rise up, so they part again. But it is not only those who meet each other during the course of life who will have to try and find out whether what arises within them can provide sufficient basis for an ongoing relationship. Sons and daughters, too, will find it increasingly difficult to understand fathers and mothers, parents will find it harder and harder to understand their children, and the same will be the case for sisters and brothers. Mutual understanding will become increasingly difficult because it will be more and more necessary for people first of all to let what lives in them karmically emerge properly from the depths of their being.

So you see what a negative prospect is opening up for the fifth post-Atlantean epoch—the prospect of difficulties in mutual understanding amongst human beings. We are challenged to look this evolutionary necessity squarely in the face instead of remaining dreamily in the dark, for it is, in fact, entirely necessary for our evolution. If humanity in the fifth post-Atlantean epoch were not faced with this prospect of having difficulty in mutual understanding, the consciousness soul would be unable to develop. The consequence of this would be that people would have to live collectively more on the basis of natural instincts. The individual aspects of the consciousness soul would be unable to develop; so it is essential for humanity to undergo this trial.

It is important to face up squarely to the whole situation, for if the negative side of evolution in the fifth post-Atlantean epoch were to develop alone war and conflict would be unavoidable even in the most petty situations. So we see that certain requirements are beginning to arise instinctually of which we must become increasingly aware, and it is one of the tasks of spiritual science in the fifth post-Atlantean epoch to help human beings become more and more conscious of these.

4.6.2 The consequences of deeds of love and deeds of duty

Now we can trace how an impulse from one life works on into other lives. Take, for example, the impulse of love. We can do our deeds in relation to other human beings out of the impulse which we call love. It makes a great difference whether we do them out of a mere sense of duty, convention, respectability and so on, or whether we do them out of a greater or lesser degree of love.

Let us assume that in one earthly life a human being is able to perform actions sustained by love, warmed through and through by love. It remains as a real force in his soul. What he takes with him as an outcome of his deeds, what is now mirrored in the other souls, comes back to him as a reflected image. And as he forms from this his astral body, with which he descends onto the earth, the love from the former earthly life, the love which he poured out and which was now returned to him from other souls, is changed to joy and gladness.

A human being does something for his fellow human beings, something sustained by love. Love streaming out from him accompanies the actions which help his fellow human beings. In the passage through life between death and a new birth, this outpouring love from the one life on earth is transmuted, metamorphosed, into joy that streams in towards him.

If you experience joy through a human being in one earthly life, you may be sure it is the outcome of the love you unfolded towards him in a former life. This joy flows back again into your soul during your life on earth. You know the inner warmth which comes with joy, you know what joy can mean to one in life—especially that joy which comes from other human beings. It warms life and sustains it—gives it wings, as it were. It is the karmic result of love that has been expended.

But in our joy we again experience a relation to the human being who gives us joy. Thus we had something within us in our former life on earth that made the love flow out from us. In our succeeding life, we already have the outcome of it, the warmth of joy, which we experience inwardly once more. And this again flows out from us. A human being who can experience joy in life again represents something for his fellow human beings—something that warms them. A person who has cause to go through life without joy is different with regard to his fellow human beings from one to whom it is granted to go through life with joyfulness.

Then, in the life between death and a new birth once more, what we thus experienced in joy between birth and death is reflected again in the many souls with whom we were on earth and with whom we are again in that life. And the manifold reflected image which thus comes back to us from the souls of those we knew on earth works back again once more. We carry it into our astral body when we come down again into the next life on earth—that is the third in succession. Once more it is instilled, imprinted into our astral body. What is it in its outcome now? Now it becomes the underlying basis, the impulse for the easy understanding of the human being and the world. It becomes the basis for that attunement of the soul which bears us along inasmuch as we have understanding of the world. If we find interest and take delight in the conduct of other human beings, if we understand their conduct and find it interesting in a given earthly life, it is a sure indication of the joy in our last incarnation and of the love in our incarnation before that. Human beings who go through the world with a free mind and an open sense, letting the world flow into them so that they understand it well—they have attained through love and joy this relation to the world.

What we do in our deeds out of love is altogether different from what we do out of a dry and rigid sense of duty. You will remember that I have always emphasized in my books: it is the deeds that spring from love which we must recognize as truly ethical; they are the truly moral deeds. How often have I indicated the great contrast in this regard between Kant and Schiller.[65] Kant, both in life and in knowledge, rigidified everything. In knowledge all became hard and angular through Kant, as it did in human action. 'Duty, thou great and sublime name, thou who containest nothing of comfort or ease . . .' and so on. I quoted this passage in my *Philosophy of Freedom* to the pretended anger (not the sincere, but the pretended, hypocritical anger) of many opponents, while over against it I set what I must establish as my view: 'Love, thou who speakest with warmth to the soul . . .' and so on.

Over against the dry and rigid Kantian concept of duty Schiller himself found the words: 'Gladly I serve my friends, yet alas, I do it with pleasure, wherefore it oftentimes gnaws at me that I am not virtuous.' For in the Kantian ethic, that is not virtuous which we do out of real inclination, but only that which we do out of the rigid concept of duty.

Well, there are human beings who, to begin with, do not

find love. Because they cannot tell their fellow human beings the truth out of love—for if you love a person, you will tell him the truth, and not lies—because they cannot love, they tell the truth out of a sense of duty. Because they cannot love, they refrain out of a sense of duty from thrashing their fellow human being directly or from boxing his ears or shoving him and so on the moment he does a thing they do not like. There is indeed a difference between acting out of a rigid sense of duty—necessary as it is in social life, necessary for many things—and the deeds of love.

Now the deeds that are done out of a rigid concept of duty, or by convention or propriety, do not call forth joy in the next life on earth. They too undergo that mirroring in other souls of which I spoke before and, having done so, in the next life on earth they call forth what we may describe like this: 'You feel that people are more or less indifferent to you.' How many a person carries this through life. He is a matter of indifference to others, and he suffers from it. Rightly he suffers from it, for human beings are there for one another; human beings are dependent on not being a matter of indifference to their fellow human beings. What he thus suffers is simply the outcome of a lack of love in a former life on earth, when he behaved as a decent man because of rigid duty hanging over him like a sword of Damocles.[66] I will not say a sword of steel, because that would be disquieting, no doubt, for most dutiful people, but a wooden sword of Damocles.

That was the second earthly life. That which proceeds as joy from love becomes in the third life, as we have seen, a free and open heart, bringing the world close to us, giving us open-minded insight into all things beautiful and good and true. While that which comes to us as the indifference of other human beings—what we experience in this way in one earthly life will make us in the next life (that is, in the third) a person who does not know what to do with himself. Such a person in school already has no particular use for the things the teachers are doing with him. Then, when he grows a little older, he does not know what to become—mechanic or privy councillor, or whatever it may be. He does not know what to do with his life. He drifts through life without direction. In observation of the outer world he is not exactly dull. Music, for instance, he understands well enough, but it gives him no pleasure. After all, it is a matter of indifference whether the music is more or less good or bad. He feels the beauty of a painting or other work of art, but there is always something in his soul that vexes him: 'What is the good of it anyhow? What's it all for?' Such are the things that emerge in the third earthly life in karmic sequence.

4.6.3 *Learning to understand karma*

What is this youth movement[67] really seeking? It is seeking to find the reality of this second, cloudlike human being who comes into evidence after puberty and who is actually there within the person. The youth movement wants to be educated in a way that will enable it to apprehend this second human being. But who is this second human being? What does he actually represent? What is it that emerges as it were from this human body in which one has observed the gradual maturing of physiognomy and gesture, in connection with which one is also able to feel how in the second period of life, from the change of teeth to puberty, pre-earthly existence is coming to definite expression? What is making its appearance here like a stranger? What is it that now comes forth when, after puberty, the human being begins to be conscious of his own freedom, when he turns to other individuals, seeking to form bonds with them out of an inner impulse which neither he nor the others can explain but which underlies this very definite urge. Who is this 'second man'? He is the being who lived in the earlier incarnation and is now making his way like a shadow into this present earthly life. Humankind will gradually learn to take account of karma from that which breaks in upon human life so mysteriously at about the age of puberty. At the time of life when a human being becomes capable of propagating his kind, impulses to which he gave expression in earlier earthly lives also make their appearance in him. But a great deal must happen in human hearts and feelings before there can be any clear recognition, any clear perception of what I have just been describing to you.

Think of the great difference there is in the ordinary consciousness between self-love and love of others. People know well what self-love is, for every individual holds himself in high esteem—of that there is no doubt! Self-love is present even in those who imagine that they are entirely free from it. There are very few indeed—and a close investigation of karma would be called for in such cases—who would dream of saying that they have no self-love in them. Love of others is rather more difficult to fathom. Such love may of course be absolutely genuine, but it is very often coloured by an element of self-love. We may love another human being because he does something for us, because he is by our side; we love him for many reasons closely connected with self-love. Nevertheless there is such a thing as selfless love and it is within our reach. We can learn little by little to expel from love every vestige of self-interest, and then we come to know what it means to give ourselves to others in the true and real sense. It is from this self-giving, this giving of ourselves to others, this selfless love, that we can kindle the feeling we must have for ourselves if we are to glimpse earlier earthly lives. Suppose you are a person who was born, let us say, in the year 1881; you are alive now. Once upon a time, in an earlier earthly life, you were born, say, in the year 737 and died in 799. The person, personality B, is living now in the nineteenth, twentieth century; formerly this personality—you yourself—lived in the eighth century. The two personalities are linked by the life stretching between death and the new birth. But before even so much as an inkling can come to you of the personality who lived in the eighth century you must be capable of loving your own self exactly as if you were loving another human being. For although the being who lived in the eighth century is there within you, he is really a stranger, exactly as another person may be a stranger to you now. You must be able to relate yourself to your preceding incarnation in the way you relate yourself now to some other human being; otherwise no inkling of the earlier incarnation is possible. Neither will you be able to form an objective conception of what appears in a human being after puberty as a second, shadowy man. But love that is truly selfless becomes a power of knowledge, and when love of self becomes so completely objective that a person can observe himself exactly as he observes other human beings, this is the means whereby a vista of earlier earthly lives will disclose itself—at first as a kind of dim inkling. This experience must be combined with the kind of observation I have been describing, whereby we become aware of the essential, fundamental nature of the human being. The urge to apprehend the truth of repeated earthly lives has been present in humanity since the end of Kali Yuga[68] and is already unmistakably evident. The only reason why people do not speak about it is because it is not sufficiently clear or defined. But let us suppose that a thoroughly sincere member of the modern youth movement were to wake up one morning and for a quarter of an hour be vividly conscious of what he had experienced during sleep, and suppose one were to ask him during this quarter of an hour. 'What is it that you are really seeking,' he would answer: 'I am striving to apprehend the whole human being, the being who has passed through many earthly lives. I am striving to know what it is within me that has come from earlier stages of existence. But you know nothing about it; you have nothing to tell me!'

In human hearts today there is a longing to understand karma. Therefore this is the time when the impulse must be given to study history in the way I have illustrated by certain examples; it is this kind of study which, if earnestly and actively pursued, will lead human beings to an understanding of their own lives in the light of reincarnation and karma.

Notes

1. *Wandervogel* movement: (literally 'migrating bird'), founded in 1901 by a Berlin school teacher and his students. Groups of adolescents and young people went camping and hiking in the countryside, getting close to nature, folk singing and dancing, optimistic and romantic.
2. *Youth and the Etheric Heart*, GA 217a, translated by C.E. Creeger, SteinerBooks, 2007.
3. Genesis: 3.
4. See Thomas Weihs, *Embryogenesis in Myth and Science*, Floris Books, 1986.
5. For evolution and the cultural epochs see for instance *Occult Science/An Outline of Esoteric Science*, GA 13, Rudolf Steiner Press, 1979/Anthroposophic Press, 1997.
6. Torquay, 11–22 August 1924, *True and False Paths in Spiritual Investigation*, GA 243, translated by A.H. Parker, Rudolf Steiner Press, 1985.
7. See Christopher Bamford's introduction to *Freemasonry and Ritual Work*, GA 265, SteinerBooks, 2007.
8. 'Totengedenken—Elsa Kriewitz' by Conrad Schachenmann, *Mitteilungen IV*, 1993, No. 186.
9. From *Mysteries of the East and of Christianity*, GA 144, translation revised by C. Davy, Rudolf Steiner Press, 1972.
10. *A Christian Rosenkreutz Anthology*, ed. Paul M. Allen, Lindisfarne/Floris Books, 2007.
11. For instance Berlin, 23 October 1905, in *The Temple Legend*, GA 93, tr. J. Wood, Rudolf Steiner Press, 1997.
12. See note 5.
13. Quoted in Peter Selg, *Unbornness*, tr. Margot Saar, SteinerBooks, 2010.
14. Arthur Schopenhauer (1788–1860), leading German philosopher of the will and the unconscious.

15. I.e. the stages of evolution known as Old Sun, Old Moon. See note 5.
16. See note 15.
17. Thorsens, 1993.
18. Rosa Mayreder (1858–1938), Austrian writer and feminist, friend of Rudolf Steiner, *Zur Kritik der Weiblichkeit* (A Survey of the Woman Problem), 1912.
19. Otto Weininger (1880–1903), Austrian philosopher, published *Geschlecht und Charakter* (Sex and Character) in 1903, in which he describes women as passive, unproductive and amoral unless they are 'masculine' women. A converted Jew, he also saw Jewishness as 'feminine'.
20. Johann Gottlieb Fichte (1762–1814), German philosopher, founder of German idealism.
21. *Juno Ludovisi*—a colossal Roman marble head of the first century AD representing the goddess Juno (Hera). It became part of the collection formed by Cardinal Ludovisi.
22. J.W. von Goethe (1749–1832), *Faust*, Part II, closing words.
23. Helena Petrovna Blavatsky (1831–91), founder of the Theosophical Society in 1875, of which Rudolf Steiner was still a member in 1906.
24. Note by Rudolf Steiner: 'This statement met with objections immediately this book was first published (1894). It was said that within the circumstances relating to her sex, a woman is able to shape her life as individually as she likes—far more freely than a man who is already de-individualized, first by school and later by war and profession. I am aware that this objection will be voiced today [1918], perhaps even more strongly. Nonetheless, I feel bound to let my sentences stand, and hope that there are readers who recognize how utterly objections of this kind go against the concept of freedom developed in this book, and who will judge what I have said by criteria other than a person's de-individualization through school and profession.'
25. It is important to remember that Steiner was saying this in 1922.

25a. See note 43.

26. From Greek mythology: Uranus, god of the starry sky, and Gaia, the earth goddess who gave birth to him.

27. See note 19.

28. *Theosophy*, tr. C.E. Creeger, Anthroposophic Press, 1994/M. Cotterell, A.P. Shepherd, Rudolf Steiner Press, 1973.

29. *The Education of the Child*, GA 34, various translations, Anthroposophic Press, 1996.

30. Kamaloca—purgatory—the first stage of the afterlife in which we experience our wrongdoings.

31. The spiritual record of all human deeds.

32. Numa Pompilius (753–673 BC), the second king of Rome, succeeded Romulus. Said to have been taught at night by the goddess Egeria on how to establish the proper sacred rites for Rome.

33. It is unclear what Steiner is referring to here—it could be ritual magical practices as he has just alluded to Freemasonry.

34. *Knowledge of the Higher Worlds/How to Know Higher Worlds*, GA 10, tr. D.S. Osmond, C. Davy, Rudolf Steiner Press, 1976/C. Bamford, Anthroposophic Press, 1994.

35. Sigmund Freud (1856–1939), psychiatrist and founder of psychoanalysis.

36. Joseph Breuer (1842–1925), see Steiner's *An Autobiography/ The Course of My Life*, GA 28, chapter 13, SteinerBooks, 2006.

37. Berlin, 4 November 1910, *A Psychology of Body, Soul and Spirit (The Wisdom of Man)*, GA 115, Anthroposophic Press, 1999.

38. Sigmund Freud, *Totem and Taboo*, tr. J. Strachey, Routledge & Kegan Paul Ltd., 1950. In the journal *Imago*, Vols I and II (1912 and 1913), these articles appear under the title 'Some Correspondences in the Inner Life of Savages and Neurotics'.

39. Gap in the shorthand report.

40. Freud dealt with the Oedipus complex for the first time in *The Interpretation of Dreams*, tr. J. Strachey, Chapter V, Section D, Avon, New York 1965.

41. Freud, *Totem and Taboo*, p. 16.

42. Otto Rank (1884–1939), Austrian psychoanalyst and one of Freud's closest colleagues.

43. Moritz Benedikt (1835–1920), physician and criminal anthropologist. From *Aus meinem Leben, Erinnerungen and Erörterungen*, Vienna 1906, Vol. 2, p. 162.

44. Sandor Ferenczi (1873–1933), a favourite pupil of Freud's who later went his own way in psychoanalysis.

45. Freud, *Totem and Taboo*, p. 131.

46. No evidence has been found that this ever took place.

47. This refers to an office that would have been held by Alice Sprengel in Steiner's intended Foundation (*Stiftung*) for Theosophy, Art and Style, 1911. See Berlin, 15 December 1911, *The Stiftung of 1911*, tr. G.F. Karnow, Mercury Press, Spring Valley 1991.

48. Plutarch (*c.* AD 46–*c.* 119), Greek biographer and writer. In *On Isis and Osiris* he makes the distinction between the two on the basis of the origin of Venus and Amor. He uses the Greek *Eros* for *Amor*.

49. For instance in Berlin, 14 May 1912, *Earthly and Cosmic Man*, GA 133, Rudolf Steiner Publishing Co., London 1948.

50. Fritz Mauthner (1849–1923), linguistic philosopher, best known for his *Beiträge zu einer Kritik der Sprache* (A Critique of Language), 3 vols 1901–02.

51. The quotations are from Mauthner's *Wörterbuch der Philosophie*, 2 vols 1910.

52. Lou Andreas-Salomé (1861–1937), German writer and friend of Nietzsche and Rilke, with connections to Freud and psychoanalysis.

53. Lou Andreas-Salomé, *Friedrich Nietzsche in seinen Werken* (Friedrich Nietzsche in his Writings), 1894.

54. Arthur Schopenhauer, *The World as Will and Representation*, tr. F.J. Payne, Falcon's Wing Press, Colorado 1958, Vol. II, Addenda to Book 4, Chapter 4.

55. See note 5.

56. See note 34.

57. Kundalini fire or light—'serpent' energy arising in the spinal column. Steiner later abandoned the Indian-Theosophical term for 'force active in spiritual power of perception' and 'an element of higher matter'. See for instance lecture in Berlin, 26 September 1905, *Foundations of Esotericism*, GA 93a, tr. J. and V. Compton-Burnett, Rudolf Steiner Press, 1983.

58. Meister Eckhart (*c.* 1260–1326), John (Johannes) Tauler (*c.* 1300–61), German mystics.

59. *Four Mystery Dramas*, GA 14, tr. R. and H. Pusch, Rudolf Steiner Press, 1997.

60. Genesis 3:7.

61. Rudolf Steiner was still a member of the Theosophical Society in 1907.

62. Testing two cross-over qualities that are inseparably bound up with one another. Either both are present or neither, so that one need only search for one of them. The method goes back to Francis Bacon.

63. See note 34.

64. See note 58. Emanuel Swedenborg (1688–1772), physician and mystic.

65. Immanuel Kant, *Kritik der Praktischen Vernuft* (Critique of Practical Reason), see *The Philosophy of Spiritual Activity*, Chapter 9. Friedrich Schiller (1759–1805), German romantic playwright and author.

66. Sword of Damocles: Graeco-Roman story as told for instance by Cicero (106–43 BC), *Tusculan Disputations V*. Damocles, who envied the ruler Dionysius of Syracuse's rich and comfortable life, was made aware of a sharp sword suspended above Dionysius's head by a horsehair.

67. See note 1.

68. Kali Yuga, 3101 BC–AD 1899, 'Dark Age', oriental esoteric term for period of evolution.

Sources

1. The Division into Two Sexes and Reproduction

1.1   Berlin, 8 December 1908, 'Original Sin' from *The Being of Man and His Future Evolution*, GA 107, translated by Pauline Wehrle, Rudolf Steiner Press, 1981.

1.2   *Cosmic Memory*, GA 11, from chapters 10 and 18, translated by Karl E. Zimmer, Rudolf Steiner Publications Inc., New Jersey 1959.

1.3   Ibid, from chapter 7.

1.4   Budapest, 7 June 1909, in *Rosicrucian Esotericism*, GA 109/111, translated by D.S. Osmond, Anthroposophic Press, New York 1978.

1.5   Oxford, 22 August 1922, in *Planetary Spheres and their Influence on Man's Life on Earth and in Spiritual Worlds*, GA 214, translated by George and Mary Adams, Rudolf Steiner Press, 1982.

1.6   Munich, 5 June 1907, from *Rosicrucian Wisdom*, GA 99, translation revised by J. Collis, Rudolf Steiner Press, 2005.

2. Male and female

2.1   Munich, 18 March 1908, 'Man and Woman in the Light of Spiritual Science', GA 56, *The Anthroposophical Review*, Vol. 2, No. 1, Winter 1980, translated by Bernard Jarman.

2.2   Dornach, 4 January 1922, *Soul Economy and Waldorf Education*, GA 303, translated by Roland Everett, Rudolf Steiner Press/Anthroposophic Press, 1986.

2.3   Stuttgart, 16 June 1921, *Waldorf Education for Adolescence*, GA 302, Rudolf Steiner Press, 1980.

2.4   Ilkley, 8 August 1923, *A Modern Art of Education*, GA 307, translation revised by J. Darrell, Rudolf Steiner Press, 1981.

2.5   Hamburg, 17 November 1906, *Woman and Society*, GA 54, Rudolf Steiner Press, 1985.

2.6   From *The Philosophy of Spiritual Activity*, chapter 14, GA 4, translated by Rita Stebbing, Rudolf Steiner Press, 1992.

3. Sex and its attendant problems

3.1.1 Stuttgart, 21 June 1922, *Adolescence—Ripe for What?*, GA 302a, translated by M. Stott, Steiner Waldorf Schools Fellowship, 1996.

3.1.2 Dornach, 31 July 1916, *The Riddle of Humanity*, GA 170, translated by J.F. Logan, Rudolf Steiner Press, 1990.

3.2.1 Munich, 25 August 1913, *Secrets of the Threshold*, GA 147, Anthroposophic Press/Rudolf Steiner Press, 1987.

3.2.2 Berlin, 22 March 1909, *The Deed of Christ and the Opposing Spiritual Powers*, GA 107, translated by D.S. Osmond, Steiner Book Centre, North Vancouver 1976.

3.2.3 Cologne, 8 May 1912, 'Ancient Wisdom and the Heralding of the Christ Impulse', GA 143, *Anthroposophical Quarterly*, Vol. 18, No. 1, Spring 1973, translated by D.S. Osmond.

3.3.1 Hamburg, 19 May 1910, *Manifestations of Karma*, GA 120, translation revised by H. Hermann-Davey, Rudolf Steiner Press, 2000.

3.3.2 Bergen, 11 October 1913, *Links Between the Living and the Dead*, GA 140, translated by D.S. Osmond and C. Davy, Rudolf Steiner Press, 1973.

3.3.3 Nuremberg, 10 February 1918, *The Dead Are With Us*, GA 182, translated by D.S. Osmond, Rudolf Steiner Press 1985.

3.4.1 Dornach, 5 January 1918, *Ancient Myths*, GA 180, translated by M. Cotterell, Steiner Book Centre, North Vancouver 1971.

3.4.2 Zürich, 9 October 1918, 'The Work of the Angel in Our Astral Body', GA 182, from *Angels*, translated by P. Wehrle, Rudolf Steiner Press, 1996.

3.5   Dornach, 13, 15 and 16 September 1915, *Community Life,*

Inner Development, Sexuality and the Spiritual Teacher, GA 253, translated by C.E. Creeger, Anthroposophic Press, 1991.

3.6.1 From *How to Know Higher Worlds,* Chapter six, GA 10, translated by C. Bamford, Anthroposophic Press, 1994.

3.6.2 Landin, 29 July 1906, *The Christian Mystery,* GA 97, translated by A.R. Meuss, Completion Press, Gympie 2000.

4. Love

4.1.1 Zürich, 17 December 1912, *Love and its Meaning in the World,* GA 142, translated by D.S. Osmond, E.F. & S. Derry, Anthroposophic Press, 1998.

4.1.2 Nuremberg, 2 December 1911, 'Faith, Hope, Love', from *Esoteric Christianity,* GA 130, translation revised by M. Barton, Rudolf Steiner Press, 2000.

4.1.3 *The Philosophy of Spiritual Activity,* chapter 1, GA 4, translated by R. Stebbing, Rudolf Steiner Press, 1992.

4.1.4 Kassel, 29 June 1907, in *The Secret Stream,* GA 100, Anthroposophic Press, 2000.

4.2.1 Berlin, 22 November 1906, 'The Origin of Evil' from *Supersensible Knowledge,* GA 55, translated by R. Stebbing, Anthroposophic Press/Rudolf Steiner Press, 1987.

4.2.2 Berlin, 1 April 1907, *Original Impulses for the Science of the Spirit,* GA 96, translated by A.R. Meuss, Completion Press, Lower Beechmont 2001.

4.2.3 Berlin, 12 June 1907, as above.

4.2.4 Stuttgart, 14 June 1921, *Anthroposophische Grundlagen für ein erneuertes christlich-religiöses Wirken,* GA 342, Rudolf Steiner Verlag, 1992. Translated by Christian von Arnim for this volume. See also *First Steps in Christian Religious Renewal,* SteinerBooks, 2010.

4.3 Hamburg, 27 May 1910, *Manifestations of Karma,* GA 120, translation revised by H. Hermann-Davey, Rudolf Steiner Press, 2000.

4.4.1 Dornach, 6 December 1918, 'Social and Antisocial Instincts', from *The Challenge of the Times*, GA 186, translated by O.D. Wannamaker, Anthroposophic Press, 1941.

4.4.2 Berlin, 20 February 1917, *Cosmic and Human Metamorphoses*, GA 175, Anthroposophical Publishing Co., London 1926.

4.5   Dornach, 22 July 1923, 'The Spiritual Perspective' from *What is Anthroposophy?* GA 225, translated by C. Bamford and M. Spiegler, Anthroposophic Press, 2002.

4.6.1 Zürich, 10 October 1916, *Psychological Distress and the Consciousness Soul*, from *The Meaning of Life*, GA 168, translated by J. Collis, Rudolf Steiner Press, 1999.

4.6.2 Dornach, 24 February 1924, *Karmic Relationships*, Vol. I, GA 235, translated by G. Adams, Rudolf Steiner Press, 1972.

4.6.3 Breslau, 12 June 1924, *Karmic Relationships*, Vol. VII, GA 239, translated by D.S. Osmond, Rudolf Steiner Press, 1973.

For discussions of some of these themes, including homosexuality, see also articles in *The Anthroposophical Review*, Vol. 5 No. 3 1983, *Moral Freedom and Modern Dilemma*, as well as further articles on male and female in the issue cited above.